I WANT ONE VOLUNTEER

ERNEST G. BLACK

D1542950

THE RYERSON PRESS, TORONTO

Printed and bound in Canada by The Ryerson Press

I WANT ONE VOLUNTEER

Contents

1: The Excuse

And oftentimes, excusing of a fault
Doth make the fault the worse by the excuse.
WILLIAM SHAKESPEARE

In my family there is a tradition about great-great—I have forgotten how many greats—grandfather Godfrey who carried a musket in the War of 1812. That is almost all that I know about him. Often I have wished that there were some letters or other writings still treasured in the family that would give me some idea of the life of militiamen in the field in those days, how they lived, what they were fed, the nature of the discipline they were subjected to, and how it felt to serve beside regular troops who were probably among the first to use the phrase "bally colonials." I would love to know if he saw action and was at Queenston Heights and Lundy's Lane or if he spent his days in the service on guard duty at some supply depot.

I do know, however, that he was a credit to his United Empire Loyalist family of puritans. He refused to drink his rum issue. That is something that his family boasted of for generations and that probably, and not the fact that he saw service, is why he has been remembered. That, and the creditable fact much cherished in the family tradition that although he would not drink the vile stuff my thrifty ancestor drew his ration and sold it to his comrades. The pledge that little boys took in those days was probably not the one that was extorted from me as soon as I could toddle to "taste not, touch not, handle not."

I know also that grandfather Godfrey died of tuberculosis not long after the war. I wonder sometimes if that would have happened if he had had his little tot of rum before rolling up in his blankets in a wet hayfield or burrowing into a musty haymow with nothing to keep him warm but thoughts of the pennies he had in his pocket from the sale of his rum issue. I do not even know if he had a blanket. Perhaps he rolled up in his greatcoat as his descendant did on many occasions one hundred years later.

One reason, then, for these pages is my grandchildren and their grandchildren. I want them to know what World War I meant to their grandfather in addition to the fact that he was in the army, did not get a medal and was not shot for desertion.

Another part of my excuse is my old gang. For years members of the batteries in which I served have hinted that someone ought to write a history of those batteries. No one has taken the hint. This is not a battery history. There is no consecutive narrative. I have tried to show what life was like in the army by a number of scenes grouped together by subject but quite independent of their place in time. That is the way we tell each other our stories at our reunions. I hope that my pals will not mind hearing some of my stories again.

So these pages, in part and no small part, are for my comrades-in-arms. There is no tie in the world, aside from the family tie, which is quite like the tie of brothers-in-arms.

You can talk about your club or your classmates or your lodge or your fraternity. They are fine but the tie of brothers-in-arms goes deeper than any of them and has elements of all of them, and more. It is the tie of men who have lived and toiled and cursed and quarrelled together for months and years, who have stolen each other's blankets and nickel-bits and spurs and yet knew that it was safe to leave a wallet or a watch unguarded on a bunk; who went on leave together and who drank all that was good for them together in the same pubs and *estaminets;* groused together on the bleak winter nights on guard or piquet duty; and then when the time came worked together like a team while coalboxes exploded around the gun-pits and sometimes in the gun-pits; yes, and sometimes put on field dressings and carried each other to the dressing station, or wrapped a rubber groundsheet around a buddy and fired a shot over him as he was buried in the mud.

The tie is kindred to the mediaeval relationship of blood brothers, which Shakespeare expresses when he makes King Henry say before the battle of Agincourt,

> We few, we happy few, we band of brothers;
> For he today that sheds his blood with me
> Shall be my brother.

If you want to get some idea of what the tie means to veterans get yourself smuggled into a reunion dinner sometime. They are really jolly and boisterous affairs albeit they are not quite as noisy as they used to be when we were younger. There is one pause that you will never forget, when we remember our fallen comrades. Some units start proceedings with two minutes silence. My outfit treats it as a toast, immediately after The Queen.

No matter how noisy and jolly the party and no matter how tipsy a few may appear, when the toastmaster rises after The Queen there is a silence that is almost unbearable after the din that has preceded it. The toastmaster says simply, "Fallen Comrades." We rise and stand at attention. A trumpeter blows the Last Post. As the call proceeds the lights go out one by one, until by the time it is completed we are in total darkness. For two minutes we stand motionless at attention in the dark. What do we think of as we stand there? Is it Speedy, lying face down in the mud at Passchendaele, or the hand we buried at Ypres under the cross marked *Jimmie Jones,* or is it the "Mother" coming in red bubbles through the lips of poor old Monty in Vimy Square? Perhaps it is of pals who have dropped out since the war. Time is more deadly than war. Many more have answered the last roll-call since the armistice than fell in over two and a half years at the front.

There are not many of us left, just enough for a good reunion. Our circle is getting smaller, but as the gaps come we close up and we find that we are closer to each other now than we ever were before.

After the two minutes' silence the trumpet blows Reveille and the lights come on one by one, so that the room is fully lighted by the time the call is completed. Then we raise our glasses and without drinking say, "Fallen Comrades," those of us, that is, who can get the words out with lumps in our throats as big as footballs.

These pages are also for myself. It seems odd that my memories of a thing so horrible and inhuman as World War I should almost all be pleasant. I remember a comic post-card that I saw as a boy. It depicted a harassed man in a nightshirt, walking the floor with a bawling infant in his arms. In the background was a clock that read two-thirty. Underneath were the words, "A million wouldn't buy you, baby, but not a nickel for another one like you." That expresses my feelings with reference to war memories.

Occasionally I dream about the war. All of those dreams have been pleasant except one. In my only nightmare in scores of dreams about the war in nearly fifty years I dreamed that I was back in the army, and lousy. That woke me up and it was long before I went back to sleep. Usually when I dream of the war I go through the whole of it. I start in training camp and go all the way to the end. Often I win the war single-handed. Once I was in a trench that the Germans had reached with a tunnel. They were attempting to come through to take over our trench. As each man appeared I hit him over the head with the edge of a shovel. Then I dropped the shovel, grabbed the German by the shoulders and pulled him through the hole into our trench, where I piled him on his fellows. Then I picked up the shovel and attended to the next customer. Before I awoke I had Germans piled so high that I could not see the sky.

Perhaps a psychologist can tell you what that dream indicates about my character. I do not care: all I know is that I had a whale of a time.

Most of these pages will be about pleasant things. With such a backdrop as World War I there will of course be unpleasant things intruding. That cannot be helped. All I can hope is that the reader will have half as much fun in the reading as I have had in the writing. Perhaps in selecting a name I should have borrowed from Bennett Cerf and called this book *Try and Stop Me.*

2: Rats and Other Things

Quoth Hudibras, "I smell a rat!"
SAMUEL BUTLER

When we first arrived in France in the early summer of 1916 groups of us were sent up the line to be attached to batteries in action for a few days to get the feel of things. Some of us went to a Second Division battery on the shore of Dickebusch Lake a short distance south of Ypres. Most of the guns in the area were under direct observation by the Germans on a sizable knoll just south of the salient. Not only could they see us but on clear mornings they probably knew what we had for breakfast. From time to time, even when the front was quiet, they would take a shot or two at us just to show that they knew where we were and that we were not forgotten.

The first morning we were there I was outside the gun-pit when the daily shoot took place. It was a pleasant summer morning and there were a number of gunners outside with me. I got my first lesson in what to do under shellfire. At the sound of the first approaching shell almost everyone went flat. I was the last one to go flat, from pure ignorance. The only one who did not go down at all was a battery corporal who took shelter instead of going flat. Taking shelter was an excellent protective movement if the shelter was adequate. The shelter the corporal took was not well chosen and is not recommended; it was a nice bushy hedge but rather insubstantial. He ran into it with his head down and his rear end up. That is where he got the Blighty, in the seat of his pants.

It was a lovely Blighty, a nice splinter in the fleshy part of his rear end, nothing to do any permanent damage but enough to get him to hospital in England and a furlough before he came back to France. During dull moments in the gun-pits we often killed time by debating the question of how badly we would be willing to be hit to get a Blighty. It was similar to the question of how much of a leg you would give for a V.C. That discussion was brought to a close by a very sensible Irishman who said, "Not so much as me big toe." That is very different from something I read in Lord Ismay's memoirs. He tells with obvious approval of the grizzled old general who said, "I would welcome a post-humous V.C." None of us was old enough to pay that price.

That was my baptism of fire. At that position I saw something else for the first time. The gun-pits we were visiting were comfortable and reasonably protected from shellfire except direct hits, but they were not roomy and they had no guest-rooms. Fortunately there was an abandoned battery position a few yards away and we visitors slept there. The first morning in those gun-pits I woke to see something sitting up in the doorway regarding us intruders with obvious disapproval. It was a big Belgian rat sitting upright with its paws up like a rabbit and almost as large as a rabbit. I said Belgian rat because there was a great difference in size between the rats in France and those in Belgium. The Belgian rats were nearly twice the size of their French cousins.

From then on we saw them often. They infested our gun-pits. Wherever there was food or might be food, cadavers included, they swarmed. If you hung up your tunic they ate the biscuits out of the emergency ration sewed inside the lining. That did not matter much because we soon got tired of carrying the ration around. I even killed one in bed. That was in a position we had sometime later farther north on the shores of Dickebusch Lake. There we built a little ell off the gun-pit for sleeping quarters. We acquired some lumber and built double-decker bunks, with four-by-fours as corner posts. One night, lying half asleep, I felt a rat run over me and kicked. Luckily I hit him. If I had not I might easily have broken my instep, for I caught him between my foot and one of those four-by-fours. His body broke the blow on my foot, which was lucky for me for I kicked hard enough to kill him outright.

We tried many things to get rid of them. Shooting at them was soon forbidden because there was no way of telling where a ricocheting bullet might come to rest. We tried other methods. We would scatter pieces of hardtack at night on the ground outside the gun-pits. When we heard the rats gnawing the biscuit we would rush them with electric torches to blind them and then vie with each other in seeing how far we could kick them. The old army boot was an ideal weapon for such warfare. Twenty- or thirty-foot kicks were common.

Perhaps our warfare had some success. I do not remember much about rats in the last year of the war. Perhaps we just got used to them.

With rats swarming around our lines one would expect that their traditional enemies, cats, would be there, too. I have tortured my memory trying to recall cats, almost without success. The only cat I remember was a big black one that came from nowhere and attached itself to us at the Somme. What attracted her or him, I have forgotten which, may have been scraps from our mess tins, but may have been the warm bed she discovered on our gun. When the gun was fired it slid back and then forward again on wide metal guides, which after a little firing became warm. Pussy found those guides a nice cosy bed on cold autumn nights.

One night we got a sudden order to fire in our SOS lines and went into action without thinking of pussy sleeping up front on the guides. It must have been a rude awakening when the gun slipped out from under the cat leaving her in the middle of the blast. There was a yowl we could hear above the roar of the gun and a black streak disappeared through the front of the gun-pit. We did not see pussy again for some days but eventually we were forgiven and our black cat came back to stay with us until we pulled out late in November. It was not much of a compliment to us that she preferred a battlefield to our company, but it underlines the statement often made that cats become attached to places and not to people. Pussy was a native of Martinpuich only a few yards away and had stuck it out for five months in the very heart of one of the world's greatest battles rather than leave her home.

There were things, however, to which we never did get used. They were the *cooties*, the nickname for body lice, also referred to as greybacks. Even talking of them is unpleasant, but no account of life at the front would be complete without something about them. The men in World War II were lucky; thanks to DDT, cooties were no longer a problem.

Great efforts were made to eliminate them, but in the conditions in which we lived that seemed to be an impossibility. I remember one offensive that deserved to succeed. We were in Vimy village, sleeping in a wine cellar. All our kit and belongings were removed and piled outside in the sunshine. Then we scrubbed the interior of the cellar, walls, floors and bunks with creoline. (*Creoline*, I think, was a trade name. I cannot find it in the dictionary. It was a strong antiseptic and probably contained a large percentage of creosote. We were supplied with all of it that we asked for, and it came to us in large metal drums.) Then we went outside and washed our underwear in a strong solution of creoline. After that we stripped off our uniforms and sponged them inside and out with the same solution. The seams, which were the depositories of the nits, were treated with almost pure creoline, so strong in fact that if one perspired in the next few days there were likely to be blisters. Last of all we went after our blankets. First they were given a good shaking, then spread in the sun and sprinkled with creoline. When they were almost wet with the stuff they were rolled up tight to give it a chance to work. That night our cellar was rank with the smell of creoline and our blankets were still damp with it. It had an acrid and, most people would say, unpleasant smell but we liked it. It meant that for a day or so we would be free of the little greybacks. What did it matter if we did burn and blister from the stuff we had drenched into the seams of our uniforms?

Sometimes we gave up the fight. We did that at Passchendaele. In the six weeks we were there I never had my clothes off even once. When at the horse lines there, I slept on the floor of a four-man hut. There was a home-made stove on a rock in the middle and two men slept on each side of it. My sleeping companion and I had an arrangement by which we would lie back to back with my knees braced against sandbags of the outer wall and his knees braced against the rock under the stove. Then we would scratch backs.

The day we left there I remember riding along in a cold December wind with the front of my tunic open so that I could capture the older and larger of my inhabitants and drop them out on the road. When we got to our rest position at Verdrel we were among civilians and had the unusual opportunity to patronize a local washerwoman. Usually we did our own washing. The old lady brought back our washing with the terse comment, in what passed between the army and the civilians as French: *Beaucoup itchycoo.*

Someone has described St. Thomas à Becket in a serge blouse so heavy with vermin that you could see the cloth move. I can understand that description. I saw one of the cooks in Vimy village sitting in his undershirt in bright summer sun outside his dug-out. In his hands was a heavy turtleneck sweater, which he had turned inside out. The sweater was dark blue but there were large patches of it on which you could not see even a trace of the blue through the masses of greybacks on it.

Located in some spots in our uniforms cooties were infuriating. Artillerymen wore riding breeches that fitted closely at the knees. A few cooties lodged in the tight part where they could not be reached, just inside the bend of the knee, would drive one to distraction. A favourite place was in the ribs of

10

woollen socks, just behind the ankle. There they were hell on earth. You could take the sock off and search it carefully but when you put it on again the pests were still there. A common sight at night was some cursing gunner running the flame of a candle along the seams on the inside of his uniform where the little white nits turned the khaki grey. They would snap and crackle like popcorn but one never seemed to get all of them.

The hot-stove league existed long before the day of hockey broadcasts. If we had a stove with a top on it we would sit around it in the evening talking with our tunics open, while we fished out our guests and dropped them on the top of the stove. A big greyback exploded with a very satisfactory *pop*. If the stove was a brazier and had no top we just dropped them in the flames. That was not quite so good because then there was no *pop*.

One of our signallers with a statistical turn of mind (he taught mathematics after the war) made a personal census at the Somme. He was at the observation post and at the time had nothing to do and nothing to read. Boredom was not the least of the horrors of war. He killed time by stripping off and making a count. I have forgotten the exact figures but they were something like this: undershirt, four hundred; drawers, three-hundred and eighty. That would be far from a complete count, however, for newly hatched ones were almost invisible. And being young and ambitious with their way to make in the world, those little ones gave the most trouble. The census did not include his socks or his uniform.

One of the things we resented about our officers was the fact that for the most part they managed to keep clear of the little pests. Usually they had better quarters than we had and each of them had a batman, or personal servant, who except on a very busy front had nothing to do but look after his officer and his equipment. One of our gunners felt that very keenly and, having a grudge against one of the officers, long since dead, took steps to rectify what he felt was an injustice. First he got a round cigarette tin with a capacity of about half

11

a waterglass. Then he made a personal clean-up, dropping each of the captives into the tin until it was about three-quarters full. Watching his opportunity he sneaked into the officers' quarters and distributed the contents of the tin thoroughly through the officer's blanket roll. We were all in on the secret and watched the officer hopefully for some days for evidence of the result. We were disappointed. That officer must have been a descendant of the clan of the Spartan boy who let the fox eat out his vitals rather than betray its presence in his clothing by any outcry. Not once did we see him scratch himself on parade. We did notice, however, that for some time his batman had less idle time on his hands than was usual on a quiet front.

There were times when we managed to keep fairly clean. That was when we had a long spell in good quarters on a quiet front. One such period was in front of Vimy after we came out of the Somme. There we had a gun position that had been built by the French engineers before the British took over that part of the front. There was a deep trench behind the gun-pits cut well down into the chalk. The gun-pits were roomy and well covered with sandbags. Beside the gun-pits were dug-out sleeping quarters, reached from the bottom of the trench by a stair of fourteen steps. Inside the one for my gun there were permanent bunks and a centre space with a home-made table and a couple of easy chairs from the Monastery of Mont St. Eloi just behind us. There was an open fireplace topped by a chimney bored to the surface through the chalk. Inside the fireplace there was an iron fire-basket also snitched from the Monastery. You will hear of that dug-out again in several places.

We were there from mid-December until early in February, when we were pulled out for rest before going back in again nearby to take the Ridge. That was probably the longest period we had in France without too much trouble from vermin. We scrubbed the place with creoline, sprinkled our blankets, swabbed the inside of our uniforms and washed our underwear. We all had two suits of underwear, one on and the other, reasonably clean, in our kit-bags. At the first sign of trouble we put on the spare suit and washed the discarded one in creoline. You will believe me when I say that the predominant odour in the dug-out was creoline. For all its acrid odour, creoline has pleasant connotations for us. Even now, if I smell anything resembling it I have a sense of well-being and comfort.

Just before we left that position I had a warning itch and made a change. The suit I took off was well washed and left overnight standing in a canvas water-bucket in the trench to let the creoline work. In the morning there was ice in the bucket and I left it in the trench. In a couple of days the bucket contained a suit of underwear in a solid block of ice.

I looked at it in disgust and left it in the trench expecting that in due course it would thaw out. A few days later we were pulled out of the line. My gun went proudly along the road with a canvas water-bucket dangling from its muzzle containing a block of ice, some creoline and a very sanitary suit of underwear.

You will in due course hear how I rejoined the battery on its way home after I had gone to London on leave after the armistice. As word had reached the battery that I would not be back, the part of my kit that I had not taken with me was turned in to stores or sold to finance Brussels leaves. At Witley Camp I drew blankets from the quartermaster, and of course what I got were second-hand. With those blankets I acquired scabies, commonly known as the seven-years' itch.

I had never had it in all my time in the army, and in fact there had been very few men in the battery who did. Properly treated, it is very easily cured; neglected, it will spread rapidly and is a most tiresome thing to have. It is caused by almost microscopic insects, which burrow into the skin and cause little white sores, usually under the armpits and between the fingers where the skin is most tender. When it is between the fingers it can be communicated by a handshake.

13

The cure is simple and quick and consists simply of sulphur ointment and sulphur baths. A few days will clear it up. The remedy can, however, be overdone. A friend of mine contracted scabies on a visit to a mining camp and being told of the cure and being also tremendously embarrassed by what he had, he undertook to cure himself without seeing his doctor. He took the baths and rubbed on the ointment, but being impatient he put so much sulphur in the water that it was almost sulphur mud and he put the ointment on in layers. It seemed only to make him worse. In desperation he went at last to his doctor, who looked him over and broke the bad news. "You haven't got scabies now," he said. "What you have is sulphur dermatitis." It took months to clear that up.

My difficulty in England was that it developed just as we were about to leave for home. I had already passed the doctor. I did not dare go back for treatment, for that would have meant segregation and not going home until the next boat. There was no sulphur ointment to be had in camp or in the neighbourhood of Witley; apparently I had run into a minor epidemic.

After I got on the boat it spread rapidly. I had an inside stateroom that warmed up overnight and I scratched myself so vigorously that there was blood on those nice white sheets in the morning. I still did not dare go to the doctor for that might have meant segregation in Halifax. I did not know then how quick the cure might be and that it could have been completed during the voyage. So I sweated it out.

I arrived home late in the evening. After a short talk I asked the location of the nearest drugstore. There was one at the corner. The druggist smiled as he handed a man in uniform the things I asked for. That night I had a good sulphur bath, greased myself with the ointment and rolled up in my blankets on the sunroom floor. In a few days I was cured.

Since then I have often slept on bare rocks and sandy beaches when on a fishing trip, but not since April, 1919, have I slept on bare boards.

In a feeble effort to solve the vermin problem the army built some bathhouses. I am sure that I would not have forgotten any of my trips to them and yet, try as I can, I can only recall about four times in my thirty-one months in France that I had a bath in one of them. There was one in Poperinghe, alfresco, under some apple trees where we sat in half-barrels after we had filled them with water carried in pails, and scrubbed and warbled to our hearts' content. Not quite to our content, for the sergeant in charge shooed us out long before we were ready to go to make room for the next customers. We were allowed to stay only until the boiler we had emptied was hot again. Afterwards we went to the cinema in the town where we watched a movie and dodged a steady rain of plaster from the ceiling caused by vibration from shelling in the town. We had other chances to bathe, however, and we seldom neglected any. There were rivers and ponds. One of our boys was drowned in the Somme River near Amiens just before the big push. And those summer rains! I wonder that no painter has depicted a group of naked gunners dancing in a summer shower around a gun position.

3: The 'Orses Hate the 'Aynets

Crime, like virtue, has its degrees.
JEAN BAPTISTE RACINE

In spite of its caption this chapter is not about horses. It is concerned with crime, army crime, my own and others', not much of it very heinous.

Personally I was only up for office three times. Twice I was convicted, though I thought unjustly, and sensibly punished and once I was acquitted, though guilty. The time I got off was after armistice while we were located at Grez-Doiceaux, not far from Brussels. We got frequent forty-eight-hour passes to Brussels and on one of them I was late getting back. There were two ways to go to Brussels. One was on a narrow-gauge railway straight into the city but with innumerable stops for local traffic, and the other was on the regular railroad with a change at Wavre. When asked to explain why I was late I said simply and truthfully that I had missed connections at Wavre. I did not add the important fact that I missed my connection at Wavre because I had not got on the train at Brussels. The captain, who was holding office during the major's absence on leave, accepted my explanation with a straight face and said, "Very well, sergeant. I knew you would have an explanation." You will note that he did not say "a good explanation." It was very like Jakey Cohen, the Toronto magistrate, who, when the evidence was hardly enough to convict, would shake his finger at the accused and say, "Not guilty. But . . . *don't do it again.*"

Both the other times I appeared in office were after I had received a stripe, to point up the error in judgment that underlay the promotion. The morning after I got my first stripe and became an honest-to-goodness bombardier I was late on the reveille parade. I slipped on the end of the line just as the sergeant-major shouted, "Shun." Really it was the sort of thing that could, and should, have been overlooked. I got an extra piquet out of that and a chance to show that I held no grudge against the sergeant-major. The great man himself came into the line late that night and galloped his horse along the street of the little village where we were out on rest. We had hardly got the horse away when the major came out of his billet, hatless and tunicless, demanding to know who had galloped that horse on the hard road. Nobody knew.

My worst serious offence was after I got my second stripe. It was that offence from which the title of this chapter is drawn. I was the NCO in charge of the piquet. The duties were not onerous. The duty men had to be posted and relieved every two hours. If horses came in off special duties it was the NCO's task to see that they were properly looked after by the men on piquet. That night the ration party came back from the gun lines after one o'clock. I saw the horses watered and rubbed down and furnished with haynets. Haynets were large bags of cord with about a four-inch mesh. Horses in the army, like the men, were adequately fed but not to repletion. When the hay was gone they always felt that a little bit more would be nice. Haynets after long use, often well soaked, no doubt acquired a hay-like taste. When the hay was all eaten the horses liked to have the haynets for dessert.

In the morning there was nothing left of the haynets but the cords by which they had been tied to the piquet rope, and the horses were sucking them. I was for it. In the major's office the sergeant-major stated the nature of the case against me. He was not the sergeant-major who galloped the horse

17

but a certain gentleman of whom you will hear more later called Jerry, and also known as Black Jack and the Black Prince. After averring that I had been the NCO in charge of the piquet he added, "And 'e let the 'orses heat the 'aynets." There was no denying the charge: the 'orses 'ad hate the 'aynets. I was found guilty and received several extra piquets. You can be sure that no more 'orses hate 'aynets while I was in charge.

Orderly room anecdotes are plentiful among veterans. At almost any reunion you will see someone with two or three men in a corner where they cannot get away, listening to an account of the time when the narrator was up for office. Invariably those stories end with the statement, "The colonel said to me . . ." and, "I said to the colonel . . ." The colonel always got the worst of those exchanges. One wonders how colonels ever dared to speak harshly to men appearing before them for discipline.

An old friend of mine served in the Black Watch. Once, in England, he was escort for a prisoner charged with coming in late on a midnight pass. The culprit was an old music hall artiste and put his story over with good effect. He said he was just saying good-night to his girl when her mother put out the family cat. Surely, said the prisoner, if it was all right for a tomcat to be out all night it was proper for one of His Majesty's Highlanders to have a little liberty. The colonel laughed and meted out a light penalty, three days confined to barracks. But the escort laughed, too. For that he, too, got three days CB and spent it in the cook-house peeling potatoes in the company of the man he had escorted to office.

I was not long in the army when I got my first lesson in army ethics. I was on my first guard and came off the beat at two o'clock. I then had four hours in the guardhouse, subject to call, before going on the beat again. Twenty-four-hour guards, with their two hours on and four hours off, taught me how to get rest in catnaps. Another gunner relieved at the same time expressed a desire for a snack, a sentiment that I shared though I had no idea how it was to be gratified in the middle of the night. He led me to the cook-house. One corner, a storeroom, was partitioned off, its door secured solidly by a large padlock. Sam took out his army knife and held it poised in his right hand while he grasped the padlock with his left. Slowly he turned the padlock until he judged by the pressure on his fingers that he had the right angle. Then he tapped it smartly with the back of the knife. The padlock flew wide open, though no wider than my eyes. Inside we got a dozen eggs, two raisin pies—we used to get pie in Canada—and the makings of a pot of coffee. The padlock was replaced and closed. Back in the guardroom with the other members of the guard off duty, including the sergeant, we had a feast. The little heater in the guardroom made an excellent cookstove.

That was my first lesson but it taught me more than one thing. I learned that padlocks are not nearly as formidable as they look if one understands them; that an army knife has many capabilities undreamed of by its designer; and, most important of all, that in the army the taking of government property was not considered by the troops to be theft. That was not to be found in the King's Rules and Orders; but KR & O were not the guide to our conduct. If we had been caught we could most certainly have been punished, but not being caught we had nothing on our consciences.

There were things that could be stolen, things that were, shall I say, in the public domain. All government property was in that class, whether in stores or in the possession of someone to whom it had been issued. Some private property was in the same class. It is hard to define the limits of the rule with regard to it. Illustration may be the best form of definition. Money or watches could not be touched; liquor was the property of any man who could get his hands on it. Privately owned nickel-bits and stirrups if owned by a member of your own unit were sacred, but if the property of a stranger were legitimate loot.

19

Nickel-bits, spurs and stirrups were cherished possessions. The army issue was made of some composition that was subject to rust and tarnishing and it took a good deal of work to keep the stuff clean. No driver or mounted man was happy until he had acquired a complete set of nickel by purchase or otherwise. To admit purchase was to admit inferiority, a lack of enterprise. Our battery had its first showing of nickel shortly after we got to France. An English battery that had also just come over was near us at Poperinghe. It was commanded by a duke. That was in the days when dukes still had money. As a ducal gesture, on leaving for the front he outfitted his battery completely with nickel. Those innocent newcomers kept their nickel in the harness room. Our battery did not get all of it, most of the batteries in our brigade got their share. I never heard whether the duke replaced the missing equipment. If he did I am sure that his drivers did not leave their new nickel lying about in their harness room.

Even our officers were tainted with our doctrine regarding army property. Artillerymen of the Third Division will recall without hearing his name the battery commander who had the reputation of being the worst horse thief in the whole Canadian Army. He knew horse flesh and when he saw a good specimen he coveted it and he knew how to get it. That resulted in more shenanigans. Horses were identified by numbers burned into their hoofs, of which a record was kept. A farrier-sergeant could, and often did, burn out the old numbers and replace them with new numbers corresponding to the battery records.

The farrier's talents were not, however, reserved for officers. I know of one case at least when they were made available to the men. After the armistice there was a big black mule in the lines that was something of a problem. He was seventeen and a half hands high, which is very tall for a mule. Every inch of that height was packed with stupidity and perversity. He would not even stand still on the lines. He pulled back on his chain headstall until there was an open sore on his neck half an inch deep. His driver and the whole subsection thought that he was the incarnation of Satan. Then one day a little black mule came trotting down the road with a trailing halter. It was stopped and brought into our lines. The drivers put him beside the big black mule and compared them. They looked much alike, except that the little one stood only fourteen and a half hands, a difference of twelve inches. That did not worry anyone. The seventeen and a half hands recorded in the books was so incredibly high that it could easily be explained as a clerical error. The farrier-sergeant (for the benefit of the Provost Marshal and the Judge Advocate General, he has been dead these many years) made a very neat job of putting the big mule's number on the little mule's hoofs. The little mule was tied to the piquet line and the big mule made a short trip to a Belgian butcher. The price was six hundred francs, one hundred and twenty dollars.

You will hear more about army goods sold to civilians when I get around to telling you about leave, especially leave to Brussels after the armistice.

The fact that most of our personal effects were not in what I have called the public domain and were not properly subject to pilferage was due in great part to the strong personal bond that existed between us. I think particularly of our first Christmas in France. We came out of the Somme about December first. After rest we went back about the middle of the month into the line. Before going in we got our regular fortnightly pay of fifteen francs, plus an advance, from our reserve, of fifty francs as Christmas money. A few days before that my birthday had come and gone and in my birthday parcel from home had been a money belt. How people could think of some of the things they put in our parcels we never could figure out. I got three dollars pay every two weeks, so I needed a money belt. However I was very proud of it, put my unusual sixty-five francs in it, the whole thirteen dollars, and fastened it round my middle just under my tunic.

The day we moved in was a raw winter day with a fall of snow, amounting by the time we had reached our destination to more than an inch. To ease the work of the horses the gunners, instead of riding on the limbers as usual, had to march behind the guns. As we passed the monastery at Mont St. Eloi I felt warm from the marching and opened my great-coat and tunic, leaving the long knitted muffler, which had come in the same parcel, to protect me from the wind. When we got to the gun position I found that the scarf, working up and down as I walked, had opened my money belt and my sixty-five francs were gone. That was one of the blackest moments I had in France. I started back over the road to look for my money. I scrutinized every inch of it from La Targette where the guns were to Mont St. Eloi where I had opened my greatcoat. I asked everyone I met if they had seen any money. That was a waste of breath. Anyone who had found sixty-five francs would not have been on the road; he would have been settled cosily in one of those warm *estaminets* which were still open around Mont St. Eloi.

At last I gave up and went back to the battery. When I got down into the deep dug-out beside the gun I announced my lack of success. The boys shelled out all the money they had and made a pile of it in the middle of the table. Then they divided it six ways, an equal share for each of us. I was back in business again for Christmas.

We were not always so unselfish. I remember a pair of breeches I got near Cambrai. I needed them badly, for mine had reached such a condition that I carried a sandbag over my arm for emergencies. I certainly would not have sat down on a gun seat or anything cold without a sandbag. It was near the end of the Hundred Days and transport had been much too busy with more important things to bother with pants for gunners. Our quartermaster had nothing left that would fit me.

Our position was quite close to Cambrai. Cambrai was something to remember. For days the town had been in flames and we had before us a replica of the Israelites' cloud by day and pillar of fire by night. The city in the daytime was covered by a dense pall of smoke that rose straight up like a pillar; at night glow from the flames sent up a bright shaft of light that seemed to pierce the heavens. While we were there the Germans located us and gave us a good going-over. At dusk that night the horses came up and we were moved to a new position somewhat in the rear. The horses were scarcely gone when a shell came right into the middle of our new position. It seemed uncanny but must have been the result of some German gunner's blunder. There had been nothing in that field when we moved there in the dark. We had not yet fired a round with its revealing gun flash. The only explanation is that someone was firing by map at something that the map showed, and that he had misread his map or slipped in his calculations. The fire came as if it were directed at a crossroad, without variation, with typical Teutonic regularity, one shell a minute. You could set your watch by them.

The first shell that landed hit one of my gunners. It was a Blighty and a beauty, a nice clean flesh wound that would get him to hospital and, with convalescence, would carry him over until spring. We were still thinking in terms of a 1919 campaign. We got the wounded man away to a flank and fixed up the wound with the field dressing from the lining of his tunic. I detailed a man to walk to the dressing station with him. He refused to go.

"Last time I was in hospital," he said—he had just acquired his second wound stripe, "I didn't get a chance to take my kit, and the orderly there shaved me with a dull razor. I won't go," he declared, "until somebody gets me my razor."

By this time we had figured out the shoot and knew that it was one gun firing on the same lay at regular minute intervals. I saw my opportunity and I grasped it. "I'll get your kit," I said, "if you will trade pants with me."

He had a good pair of Bedford cord breeches, one of the last issued to our battery. We were about the same size. It was a fair proposition and he accepted. First he told me exactly where his haversack lay. I waited for the next shell to land and then, even as the clods of earth from the burst were still falling around us, I started. I had no trouble finding the haversack and was back a good twenty seconds before the next shell arrived. The wounded man and I exchanged breeches and he left for the dressing station happy in the knowledge that no orderly was going to shave him with a dull razor. I was happy in the fact that I no longer needed a sandbag to sit on.

There was one army crime that is not pleasant to think of. That has to do with self-inflicted wounds. They were often called left-hand wounds, from the fact that some of them were managed by blowing off the left hand with a rifle bullet fired along the line of the hand to destroy the fingers and ensure a discharge. Too often, however, all they achieved was a court martial, when the powder embedded in the skin disclosed the nature of the wound. A man who was only after a Blighty and a white bed for a while fired the bullet through the palm of his hand and incurred no permanent disabling injuries. We had no left-handers in our battery but we did have some self-inflicted wounds and some lead-swinging.

Lead-swinging was the army name for malingering. In our outfit we divided lead-swinging into two classes, *flanneries* and *crud*. Flanneries was the result of laziness and a desire to avoid fatigues and drills; crud, which stemmed from cowardice, was a shammed sickness to avoid duty on an active and dangerous front. The first resort of the lead-swinger was the sick parade. That usually proved to be a false hope. Unless you could show a temperature you had no hope of any prescription but "medicine and duty." Medicine meant two number 9s, a laxative compounded, we were sure, of equal parts of belladonna, strychnine and TNT. A wise M.D. did not give you the pills to take, he put them in your mouth and watched you until you had swallowed them. If you could not swallow them without water, which was seldom available, after they had been sucked a short time under the MO's eye they acted as a perfect emetic.

There were various ways of producing a temperature, but the MOs were wise to all of them. Eating soap pills would produce a temperature but it also produced other symptoms that the doctors could read like a book. A man who had eaten a soap pill was as sick as a dog even before he got his number 9s. The old business of jabbing the end of a thermometer on a lighted cigarette was not at all dependable. The chances of getting between one hundred and a hundred and four without practice were very slim. A temperature of one hundred and ten, which was likely to be the result, was looked upon with great distrust and disapproval. It might easily result in three number 9s.

One of our drivers, fed up with life in the wintertime and hopeful of getting to hospital, soaked his saddle with cold water before mounting. Someone had told him that that would produce haemorrhoids. That proved to be correct. He developed the haemorrhoids and the MO gave him a tin of salve.

Another of our drivers had sufficient influenza to get to hospital. In due course he recovered and was told that in the morning he would be on the way back to the battery. After that cosy hospital the thought of our wagon lines in winter was very distasteful. In the morning no one questioned his explanation of the condition of his knee, which was swollen and inflamed. He said that he had got up in the night and tripped and fallen. The explanation that he gave to us when he finally returned was not quite so simple. He had taken two towels and tied them around his leg, one above and the other below the knee. With a stick he had twisted the towels until almost all circulation was cut off. Then with a tablespoon in each hand he beat a tattoo on his kneecap until the desired inflammation appeared. None of us ever copied his recipe.

Both of our self-inflicted wounds were at Passchendaele.

One of them was very simple and the other was rather complicated. The simple one was a mere matter of putting a foot under the wheel of a large lorry loaded with shells. By the time we got that man to the dressing station his foot was as big as a football. We never saw him again. The other man adopted a method that required help. He took a friend with him to the piquet line late one night. He kicked one of the mules and started a noisy commotion. Then he lay flat on the ground and the friend, performing a labour of love, hit him a good clip on the ankle with the blunt side of an axe. One of the men on piquet saw it but kept his mouth shut, officially.

I had had trouble with this man before that and he was one of the two men who could, if they had dared, have charged me with infraction of KR & O for subjecting them to physical violence. The man who had his ankle broken was one of a ration party of which I had charge. He did not get up when I called him nor when I roused him the second time. When I went back a third time he told me that his boots leaked and he would perhaps get his feet wet. I had come down the night before from my second or third tour of duty at the guns, when I had not for three days had a dry stitch on me. I was still not dried out. His complaint was more than I could take. I put my big army boots to him vigorously and in the place where they did the most good. That I think was better than getting him a court martial for refusing to obey an order.

The other man on whom I had used physical violence was also kicked, but that kick was not nearly so vigorous. Before the push at Amiens we had our horse lines in Boves Wood. There I warned a ration and ammunition party late in the afternoon. One of the men did not appear and I hunted him up where he was rolled in his blankets under a tree. He was only a kid and a remount but he harboured unsuspected potentialities, as will appear in a moment. He had been out the night before on the same kind of duty and needed his sleep. When he did not appear I hunted him up once more and found him asleep again. This time I stayed with him until he had his breeches on and left in the reasonable expectation that he would follow me to the piquet line. When he still did not appear I went back and found him half-dressed and half covered by his blankets, dead to the world. Then he felt my boots, gently I think, not much more than a vigorous nudge. This time I waited for him and took him personally to his chore.

I atoned for those kicks not long after we got home when I gave character evidence for him in a police court. The little scamp had been caught in a burglary and got two years for it. Long before his term was up he was paroled and immediately got into trouble again. That time he received five years. He learned his lesson. After the second stretch he went straight and has since been quite successful in a small business.

Our only other after-the-war criminal was a college graduate and an intercollege wrestling champion. He was the strongest and perhaps the laziest man I ever knew. Once in training we were moving a gun with dragropes. He was the leadman of the three on the rope on our side of the gun. From the violent contortions we saw one would think that he was pulling the gun all by himself. The other man on our rope became suspicious of him, however, and suggested to me in a whisper that we drop the rope to see what would happen. We did. The rope sagged two feet. The men on the other dragrope and on the pole kept the gun moving, but the athlete on the front of our rope with the end of it over his shoulder and going through the contortions of heavy labour was not even carrying his share of the rope.

Towards the end of the war he nearly broke my heart. There was a shortage of doctors and a call came for all men who had done one year in medicine to report to be sent back to Canada to complete their medical course. At that time it looked as if the war might go on for a generation or more. My friend got a certificate from his college registrar showing that he had taken enough biology and physics in his four-year arts course to constitute one year in medicine. He left for Canada while we were out on rest after we broke the Hindenburg Line. The night before he left he took me out and treated me to a swell meal of eggs and chips and a bottle of wine. We had enlisted together and it broke my heart when he left for home. Somehow or other he was side-tracked in England, the armistice came along and I got home before he did.

After we had been home some years he got into trouble and was sent to jail. I visited him in the preferred-class prison where he served his sentence. "Ernie, Ernie," he exclaimed as he entered the visiting room, "this has got the army beaten forty ways. Good food, good quarters," he was in an open dormitory, "and no lice. You should try it sometime."

He was probably right about the army.

One of our worst offenders was a deserter. He never should have been in the army. In World War II he would certainly never have seen active service. Any sort of test, of which we got none, would have shown that he was quite unstable and not very bright. Every time he heard a gun go off he started for home and kept going until someone asked to see his pass. Then he was in trouble. The first time it happened we were pretty unhappy about it. We heard that he had been arrested and was about to be tried by court martial. Then a notice appeared on the bulletin board announcing his conviction and sentence of death, followed by the chilling words: *Sentence has been duly executed.* That made us feel pretty bad because we knew that the poor devil could not help it.

Then about three months later he turned up at the battery. I know that there actually were some shootings and I talked to a man who had been a member of a firing party. It was a nasty, beastly business and generally speaking quite useless. The rest of us did not need the example, and the poor fellows who were shot for the most part could not help what they did. I doubt if any man ever did his duty from fear of

28

being shot. I hope that what happened to our man happened often. It certainly happened often to him. Three times he was sentenced to be shot. Only once were we told that the sentence had been carried out. A few years ago he died peacefully in his bed not far from Toronto. I am quite sure that the fact that he was pardoned three times after sentence of death never resulted in one single man deserting or shirking his duties.

Chickens were in the public domain. Any chicken that wandered near troops met an untimely end. Even those that stayed sedately at home on their roosts were not safe. I love to think of one incident near Wallop, in England. There are three Wallops, Nether Wallop, Middle Wallop and Upper Wallop. We slept in an open field between Middle Wallop and Upper Wallop on our march back to Witley Camp from the firing range at Lark Hill. After we were properly rolled up in our blankets under the guns two of our boys went scouting. Presently they returned so laden with chickens that they could hardly walk. The cook was roused, the travelling kitchen was fired up and we had a midnight chicken dinner. One of the neighbouring batteries barbecued a calf that night. Their meal cost them much less than ours cost us.

It was not until we got back to Witley that we realized just what we had done. The bill for the chickens was made out and in due course was paid out of our battery fund. Our battery fund consisted of our share of the canteen profits, augmented by regular contributions from the Mothers' Comforts League. The League met regularly in Toronto, knitted socks, read to each other their sons' letters from the front and raised money in various ways, including monthly dues. The contents of those letters sometimes drifted back to France not infrequently causing embarrassment, as when we heard that one of our number, who had not yet been up the line, had had a horse shot under him during furious fighting of which none of the rest of us had ever heard.

The saddest part of all was that those chickens were from a

pen of pure-bred, prize, white Wyandottes. They cost the battery fund eighty pounds, nearly four hundred dollars in those days. In those days, too, a dollar was a dollar. I hope our mothers did not know that the money they scraped together to buy us comforts was used to pay for stolen chickens at almost forty dollars per chicken. I also hope that they did not know that when the major would announce on parade the receipt of a draft from the League and asked what we wanted done with it, the answer would be an almost unanimous shout of *Beer*.

A couple of years ago I was back at Wallop and got a picture of that chicken-house to show the gang at our annual reunion. When I showed the slide at our battery dinner, seated on one side of me was one of the two men who had conducted the foraging. His partner on that expedition had died just about the time I was taking the picture. On the other side was one of our sergeants. He later held what I am sure was the record for the whole Canadian Army: the sergeant-major ran him for office eight times in one day when we were at Dickebusch Lake.

After I had shown the picture I let the thief tell his story. If any reader is interested in stealing chickens I advise him to read carefully. First they provided themselves with a box of sulphur matches, those old eight-day stinkers. You may find it hard to get them nowadays. Then they found their chicken-house. There the narrator remained outside to keep watch and to receive the loot. The other man took the matches and went inside. There on a long roost were the blue-ribbon birds. A match was struck and held under the beak of the first biddy. The fumes from the match knocked the bird out completely. It was removed from the roost, its neck was wrung and it was passed out the door to the waiting guard. The process was repeated all the way down the line until the roost was cleared. And not a squawk from one of them.

When the tale was finished the sergeant sitting on my other side told his tale. After we had been in France a year he got a call to brigade headquarters in the Berthonval Farm. The colonel, later General McNaughton of whom you will hear more, came straight to the point. "I am told, sergeant," he said, "that you had a hand in that chicken episode at Wallop. Is it true?"

"Yes, sir," said the sergeant. His faults did not include lying.

"I am also told that you were brigade orderly-sergeant that night."

"Yes, sir."

"Well, then, do you think it was proper for the brigade orderly-sergeant to be sitting in the middle of the road at midnight plucking stolen chickens?"

There was no reply to the last question. The sergeant kept his stripes and got off with a hundred-franc fine.

If I told you of all the chickens and other things that were stolen from civilians there would be no room in these pages for anything else. There is, however, one more chicken story that I must tell. It happened while the battery was marching back to Arras from Amiens in 1918. What I now tell is hearsay as I was on leave. On the first night of the march my subsection found a chicken-house so well stocked that after the boys had had their midnight feed there was a surplus, a whole oat-bag in fact full of chickens. In preparing to leave in the morning they tied the oat-bag on the limber of my gun. Just before the order *Walk, march!* was due a parade of strangers appeared. The parade was headed by a staff officer with his red tabs. The others included the town major, the mayor of the town, a French liaison officer and an unidentified civilian, probably the owner of the chickens.

The visitors approached our major. After some talk they started on a tour of inspection. I wish that I could have seen it. I can imagine the scene, the parade led by Shorty, that cocky little bantam-rooster with his cap perched high to compensate for his lack of inches and his cane under his arm. They were looking for chickens. Soon they approached my gun. I am assured by my gang that they expected then that the roof would fall in. Perched high on the limber was that oat-bag, chicken necks and drumsticks bulging its sides in all directions. One look would be enough to tell the search party that the search was ended. Shorty took one look, poked the bag with his cane, said, "Oats," and passed on. The parade followed him. That night Shorty had chicken for dinner with the compliments of my gun crew. In the course in leadership in our Officers' Training Schools the first thing to teach should be what not to see. My gang would have gone to hell for Shorty.

A few years ago I was back in France revisiting the battle-fields. Things had changed so much that I needed frequent help from the natives. I would start my request for directions with the statement in my army French that I was a Canadian veteran of the First War back to try to find old gun positions and horse lines. I wish that you could have seen those peasant faces when they heard that. My wife tells me that the broad smiles that greeted that statement were the most heart-warm-ing experiences of the whole trip. It was pleasant to know that all was forgotten and forgiven, even the chickens we stole, not to mention the many other things we did that might have left them bitter. It was worth the trip just to see those beaming smiles. I wish that every veteran could see the smiles that greet a Canadian revisiting the battlefields in France.

4: We Danced in Our Saddles

Give a man a horse he can ride.
JAMES THOMSON

Make much of your horses: ONE!—one, two. That, believe it
or not, was at one time an army order. It may yet be used in
the few ceremonial cavalry units that still exist. An army
order consists of two parts, the precautionary or directive part
and the executive part. The first part is given in a loud, even
voice so that the troops know what is to be done, there is a
pause so that everyone is prepared to move in unison, and
then in a loud, raucous voice comes the last part, audible
enough to be heard in the next county and usually unintel-
ligible. On that sound everyone moves, or stands fast at his
peril.

When a mounted outfit returned to its lines after a march
or a manoeuvre it was drawn up on the parade ground pre-
paratory to dismounting. Occasionally though not often the
officer in charge, before dismounting the ride, would think of
the poor horses and have them caressed. On the order every
man leaned forward and patted his horse three times, one
long firm pat and two quick ones. The horses having been
caressed it was in order to give the command *Prepare to dismount—Shmount!*

Young people who have seldom seen a horse except at the
racetrack or in a Western movie or at a rodeo will find it hard
to realize how important the horse was to the army in the
days of World War I. Not only did he carry the cavalry
and the mounted infantry, both of which were practically

33

outdated by the time I got to the war, but he drew the guns, the ammunition wagons, most of the supplies, the ambulances, and, best of all, the travelling kitchens. It is hard to say how the war could have been fought without the horse.

One of my most vivid recollections of horses is of something that happened to me near the end of the war. After we came out of Passchendaele I was slated for my third stripe and was sent to the Imperial Artillery School at Aire for an NCO course.

At the school were two classes, one for officers and the other for non-commissioned officers. It was a refresher course, for in theory we were all trained and qualified. That was very far from being so in my case. I had joined a half-trained battery just before it went overseas. All the NCOs had been appointed and trained before I joined and I got my stripes in the field. As will appear later I had had little basic training except on the gun.

The school at Aire was a very swank affair. Aire was an old French cavalry garrison town. We were in stone barracks and were very cosy after the line, sleeping in cots with mattresses, if you can call a straw palliasse a mattress.

The first morning at Aire we had riding drill. I felt a sense of well-being. I had had a good sleep in my mattressed cot. I had had a good breakfast in a permanent mess hall, quite different from my usual breakfast from a mess tin on my knees while I sat on a gun seat or a pile of shells. I was healthy and well fed; it was six weeks at least since I had left Passchendaele and I was rested and fresh; the war must have been thirty miles away; and before I left the battery to go to the school I had been deloused and had had a bath. I had no premonition of what lay ahead of me that morning.

After the nine o'clock parade we were mounted. The school was provided with horses and guns by a battery from the line. Batteries for such service were at the school for a month and their assignment to that duty was a reward for good service.

34

My own battery was attached to the Corps Artillery School at Habarque late in 1918.

The duty battery brought us horses and lined up in front of us. On the word of command we broke ranks and got our horses. There was some confusion due to the fact that we all wanted the best-looking ones. I was rather lucky and got one that looked much better than the average and much better, certainly, than he looked a couple of hours later. Once mounted we were taken over by the riding instructor, an Imperial sergeant-major. He took us to the riding school.

It was part of the peacetime cavalry establishment. It was a large stone drill hall with tanbark under foot and with painted markings on the stone wall to facilitate the execution of fancy manoeuvres. At one end a portion had been cut off by a canvas wall painted in exact imitation of the other walls. Behind the canvas partition, as I later discovered to my sorrow, was a large contour map laid out on the ground with rising tiers of seats about it to be used by map-reading classes. Having got us inside the riding school, the sergeant-major halted the ride and broke the good news.

"You are all qualified NCOs," he said, apparently without the least idea of how far he was wrong about at least one of us. "We will just trot around a few times to warm up our saddles and then we will get in the hurdles and freshen up our jumping."

Jumping! No horse ever jumped as my heart did when I heard that. Not only had I joined a half-trained battery but immediately on our arrival in England I had been made a limber-gunner. That probably requires some explanation. A limber-gunner, so named because when the battery was moving he rode on the gun limber, was the gun-layer and also a sort of nursemaid to the gun. He cleaned the gun and made minor repairs. Because of his gun-park duties he was excused from most fatigues and nearly all drills. As a result I had been busy with my gun while the rest of the battery had been riding. My riding experience had been very limited; a few watering parades, a trip to the station when going on leave, and after I became corporal a few rides in charge of ration parties or on moves from one front to another. And now—jumping.

At first it was not as bad as I feared. We trotted around the riding school a few times and then the ride was halted and the hurdles were brought in. I eyed them with apprehension. They were much like the hurdles one sees at a horse show but not so high. On top there was a fringe to give a hedge-like appearance. We lined up in front of the hurdles and at the word of command broke off one by one, trotted forward and made the jump.

At last my turn came and much to my surprise I made it, landing nicely. Then I trotted around the school to join the line waiting for another jump. We each made three or four jumps and then the ride was halted.

"You have all done very well," said the sergeant-major. He was being polite to us for the first day. "Now we will do it with folded arms."

That sentence is short and simple. A stick of dynamite is also short and looks simple. Three times in my life, maybe four times, I had jumped a horse and that experience had all taken place in the last few minutes. Now I was asked to place the reins on my horse's neck, sit erect with my arms folded, and take my horse, or let him take me, over a hurdle that by then looked at least a foot higher than it had before. The exultation I had felt after the first jump vanished. The blood in my veins turned to water.

The ride started again. As each man jumped I held my breath. Every one of them got over and when my turn came I astonished myself by getting over, too. We made four or five jumps and were halted again. That kind, deceptively soft-spoken sergeant-major addressed us again.

"That was very good," he said. "I see that you are all well trained. We will try it now folded arms and *stripped saddles*."

That meant nothing to me. I had never even heard about it. But as I listened to the detail of the movement I realized the full horror of it. First we took our feet out of the stirrups and then crossed the stirrup leathers on the saddles in front of us. In many ways that is worse than bareback; a bareback rider grips with his knees but a well-used saddle can be an extremely slippery thing. Then we were to put the reins back on the horse's neck, sit upright with folded arms and make, or try to make, a jump.

The ones ahead of me must have made the jump without mishap. I have no recollection in the daze I was in of anything that happened before my turn. It came and I started off. We came to the hurdle and went up and over. On the way down the yellow that had been fighting its way to the surface all morning broke through, and I braced myself for the landing. I did not reach for my reins but I braced myself with my legs and my heels. On my heels were my spurs.

I should say a word about my spurs. They were the old Canadian cavalry spurs with a three-inch shank ending in a four- or five-point rowel. Some of the boys, anxious to cut a figure on leave, removed the rowels and replaced them with nickels, loosely set, which jingled beautifully when they walked. But my rowels were still there, very much there in fact, and well set. Never having been used before I got my second stripe and very seldom after that except for ceremonial parades or guards, they had had no care except cleaning. A rowel is supposed to turn so that on the application of the spurs there is a series of pricks. My rowels were rusted solid so that a touch with them was like a jab with a lethal weapon.

Thus accoutred we, my horse and I, came down from the top of the hurdle. When we landed my spurs took hold, solid, like ice tongs in a block of ice. Never having had anything like me on his back before, the horse started to buck. That may have seemed natural to the horse but it was the wrong tactic. There was no way of bucking me off with my spurs nearly meeting each other in his innards. The more he bucked the tighter I held. It was lucky for me that his repertoire did not include the manoeuvres of Rosie, the bad horse we had in England who, when she could not otherwise dismount an objectionable rider, got down and rolled or wiped him off on a fence.

Deciding at last that trying to buck me off with my ice tongs well set was getting him nowhere, the horse did the only other thing he could think of and started to run. That at least was a relief for me from the bucking. The door was shut and he could not get out of the riding school but there was lots of room inside. The school was large and the class was small so there was ample room for manoeuvre. I had no means of controlling the horse because by this time the reins were tangled with his ears. All I could do was claw for the reins and hang on for dear life with my spurs. Round and round the school we went with the sergeant-major galloping after us, roaring in a real sergeant-major voice, "Halt that man! Dismount that man!"

How I would have loved to obey that order. Many times we went around the school. Time, space, cannot be measured at a time like that. The sergeant-major had just started a movement to trap me with the other riders when the horse decided that he wanted to get out. It is just possible that he knew that one of the walls was not the same as the others. Probably it was just luck that took him to the canvas partition. With a wild dash he took me through the partition and came to a halt in the centre of the large contour map laid out on the floor. To add to the climax there was a class of officers seated on the tiered benches absorbing a lecture in map-reading from an Imperial major with staff badges.

Many hands seized my horse's bridle and I was invited to dismount. *Invited* is a euphemism for my grandchildren. Old sweats will not have to be told what the sergeant-major said. After disengaging my ice tongs I dismounted. Then the damage was inspected, to the horse I mean, not the partition or the contour map, both of which were total wrecks. The damage to the poor brute was colossal. After the horse was examined attention, naturally, was shifted to my spurs.

"Is that the kind of spurs they use in the Caneyedian Army?" roared the sergeant-major. I had to admit that they were not typical. I was then paraded under escort to the black-smith shop where the farrier-sergeant filed the points off my rowels. I have those spurs at home now, tarnished old spurs with mouldy leathers and with round knobs at the end of the shank where the rowels used to be. One result of that scrape was that when I left the school I got a good mark for horse-manship, based no doubt solely on improvement.

Often in the army we wished that there were no horses. Three times a day every day in the year, Christmas included, we groomed them whether they were dirty or not. After that we watered and fed them. Watering was not so bad; usually that included a short bareback ride. And then there was piquet duty. All night, every night, there were three men on duty in the lines. Someone had to see that the horses did not strangle themselves with their headstalls or choke themselves trying to eat the piquet rope. One had to be a real horse lover to come out of the army without hating them.

There were things worse than horses. They were the mules. We had no mules in our battery when we went to France but after we were there some time we got mules for the first-line wagons. Perhaps there was a shortage of horses. Mules were supposed to be more durable than horses. Durable is the right word for them; you could not kill them no matter how much you wanted to and tried.

Like horses, mules had to be cleaned. No one without a personal knowledge of mules will believe readily what a job it is to clean a mule that does not wish to be cleaned. A fair percentage of mules object to being cleaned. The usual protest is a mule kick. Some professional wrestlers have what they call a mule kick, but anyone who has been kicked by a mule will tell you that the wrestlers have never been able to approach the original. A mule kick is something out of this world.

When a horse kicks he usually kicks with both feet and to a certain degree has to get set for it. A mule can kick, and does, with one foot from any stance and in almost any direction.

An active mule can get a man near the front of his body with a sort of clawing motion and land him among the horses in the next piquet line. If you think that that leads to amicable relations between man and beast you are mistaken.

A common method employed in cleaning a refractory mule was to put a twitch on him. A twitch is a very simple device based on the principle that if two things are annoying you, you will give your attention to the one that is annoying you most and ignore the other. A mule does not like to be groomed and he does not like a twitch. He dislikes the twitch more than he does the grooming so he fights the twitch and ignores the grooming.

As I said, a twitch is a very simple device. It consists of a stout stick about one and a half inches in diameter and about two feet in length. A hole is bored through one end of it and through the hole is looped about fifteen inches of strong cord or light rope. The noose is put around the animal's upper lip and the stick is then turned until the rope cuts into the lip. That usually takes a mule's mind off the grooming.

Occasionally, however, a twitch was not effective. We had one mule that could not be groomed without a good firm twitch on his lip and someone twisting his tail at the same time. He was a mule with a one-track mind and nothing in the world would divert his attention from the man with the brush and currycomb. One or two drivers who thought that they had a way with a horse or a mule undertook to clean him but they all wound up in the mud behind the piquet line, or even in the next piquet line.

Desperate measures were called for and were adopted. First the mule was hobbled tightly and then thrown. With his feet tightly tied he was cleaned on one side and then rolled over and cleaned on the other side. That left a problem. Our horse lines were often muddy spots in open fields. When the mule got up the side he had been lying on last was dirty again. It looked like an endless operation. We compromised by giving the dirty side a quick rub after the mule got up, but while he was still hobbled. I say a quick rub because while on his feet, even though hobbled, there was no telling what he might do; and whatever he did would be unpleasant.

I cannot speak of mules without thinking of Happy's mule. In thinking of Happy old comrades of his always remember the corporal who used to come into the bunkhouse in England, looking for someone for a fatigue. "I want one volunteer," he would announce. "Happy, you go." And Happy always went. He was that kind. Also he was a natural-born clown with considerable talent. He drove a team of mules one of which was unusually tractable and teachable for a mule. He could ride it bareback and bridleless and control it with the pressure of his knees. He worked it into a number of skits that we thought were comical and clever. During the summer of 1918, after the Germans had made their great break-through and for a second time threatened Paris, the Canadian Corps was on a quiet front. We were being prepared for the great offensive in front of Amiens. Someone had the bright idea of having a sports contest to keep the boys happy. Each unit held its own contest and sent the winners to a brigade event. From Brigade they went on to Division and finally to the Corps games, which were held on Dominion Day. Happy entered his mule and sailed through easily as far as Division. He won there, too, but was not allowed to go to Corps because, he was told, there was not room enough on the grounds for him and his mule to perform. Perhaps something that happened at Division was the reason for that decision.

One of his stunts was a bareback ride into a crowded part of the field. Suddenly the mule stopped. Happy got off and went through the routine then common with cranky motor cars. In those days when a car would not go you had to get down on your back to examine the mechanism. Happy did that with the mule to the delight of the large crowd, including the general. After appropriate manipulations Happy climbed out from under the mule, cranked it with its tail,

41

mounted and rode off. The applause, in which the general joined, was generous.

By way of encore Happy backed up his mule in front of the general. He got off and covered the mule's rear end with a large black cloth such as photographers use in focusing. Happy got under the mule with his head between its hind legs and went through the business of focusing. When that was done he removed the cloth and, using the tuft on the end of the mule's tail as a bulb, he took the general's picture. No one enjoyed it more than the general.

That was General Lipsett. He started his military career as a private in the South African War and ended it as a major-general in charge of the Fourth Canadian Division, when he was killed near Cambrai in October, 1918. He was on a midnight reconnaissance when he was killed in No Man's Land, examining obstacles that he was about to ask his boys to overcome. For a major-general that was beyond the call of duty. I wonder how many of our generals ever saw No Man's Land except through field glasses.

But, as I said, Happy did not get to Corps. Someone perhaps had heard that General Currie, our Corps Commander, did not like posing for photographs.

Remounts always created a problem. Horses, like men, become casualties in wartime. From time to time we received replacements. (In the artillery even the replacements of men were called remounts.) When remounts arrived there was a lively time. Almost every mounted man in the battery felt that he was entitled to a better horse, or in case of the drivers two better horses. What took place was a combination of horse show, slave market and auction, complicated by matters of personal influence and loud vociferation of personal rights.

Shortly after we came out of Passchendaele we had a large bunch of remounts. Among them was a beautiful black, which drew all eyes. All the officers and NCOs were well mounted at the time except one officer who happened to be away from the lines the day the remounts arrived. The lead driver of the gun team of the subsection I was with had lost a horse at Passchendaele and made a claim. When the tumult and the shouting died he had the black. He was a real prize for a gun driver, strong, active and easy to handle in a gun team. But he had one trait that no one suspected at the time and that I will disclose now because it is the key to what followed. His gregarious instinct was overdeveloped. In other words, he was attached to the herd, and you could not ride or drive him alone or get him to leave the horse lines without the company of at least one other horse.

This happened while I was at the Army School and what I now report is purely hearsay. If I had not been away I would have seen Act I and would not have been involved in Act II. The officer who had been away when the remounts came was interested in the big black when he saw it in the lines and in harness on the gun team and he coveted it, just as I did later, both of us to our sorrow. Jinnie watched with resentful eyes as his horse was led away.

The sequel was not long in developing. The horse was saddled, the officer mounted and tried to ride out of the horse lines. No dice. Persuasion was resorted to. The officer's groom tried to drag the brute out by the bridle. Again no dice. Persuasion was applied to the other end of the horse, including a couple of good swipes with a whiffletree. As a last resort the horse was blindfolded with an oat-bag and led out onto the road. At some distance from the battery, with the horse's head turned away from our horse lines, the oat-bag was removed. Away they went at a brisk trot without meeting any traffic for a mile or so. Then they came to the horse lines of our ammunition column.

There the big black turned in to join his kind. Nothing could stop him when under the influence of his gregarious instinct and nothing that the ingenuity of the drivers at the column could devise would induce him to leave those nice horses on the column piquet line. At last the blindfold was resorted to again, and the big black and the officer were started back to our lines. Again there was no traffic on the

43

road. As they approached our lines the horse's manner changed. From a gentle trot he went up to a canter and then into a full gallop as he entered the lines and got back to the herd.

Our horse lines in that position were old ones that had been used by many units before us. There was gravel for the horses to stand on and gravel in the lane between the lines. And there was a covering for the horses, a roof to keep off the snow and rain, supported by posts that were braced at intervals by scantlings. In his anxiety to rejoin the herd the big black did not bother to find the entrance; he went in at a corner under a scantling that was just high enough from the ground to let him go under it. It was not high enough for the officer who was neatly wiped off. He landed on the seat of his smart Bedford cord breeches on a manure pile.

Jinnie got the big black horse back in his gun team.

Shortly after that I came back from the Imperial Artillery School and I had an outrider problem on my hands. When I got my second stripe and became a corporal I had taken over my predecessor's mount. He, the corporal, was a snappy little scrapper who weighed about one hundred and fifteen pounds fully dressed with his bandolier and spurs on, and soaking wet. The horse was just made for him, a nervous little bay about the size of a small thoroughbred but not large enough for a man my size and weight. At that time that did not matter much as I spent most of my time at the gun position and was seldom mounted. But now that I was a sergeant and a graduate of the Imperial Artillery School with a good mark in horsemanship, things were different. I wanted a real war horse, a deep-chested, fiery steed with arching neck and lashing tail, which would snort and paw the ground and let the world know that few men but his master could ride him.

Old Doc came to my assistance. Doc, rest his soul, was an old horseman who had spent all his life with horses. He suggested the big black. At that time I had not heard of the officer's attempt to ride him. Doc said that the black had not

44

been trained as an outrider but he was sure that he could train him. He actually said *we*, but I knew that including me in the act was just politeness. I have never blamed Doc for what happened. I am sure there was no malice in his suggesting the horse and that he was sure that he could train him.

I saw the horse and was fascinated. The first thing was to get him. In my book that meant speaking to Jinnie. I could have claimed him but I had no intention of pulling rank to get him, so I spoke to Jinnie, with what soft-soaping palaver I have forgotten now. I was surprised at how easily I succeeded. Perhaps that should have been a warning to me.

"Sure, sarge," said Jinnie. "Sure you can have him." Jinnie no doubt had vivid recollections of what had happened to the last person who had tried to hijack his horse. No doubt he looked forward with anticipation to what he knew was bound to happen, confident that in a short time the black would be back in his gun team. I am not so sure that Jinnie was as free from malice as was Doc. I am not sure, considering everything, that I blame him.

A few days later we had a quiet half-day and Doc and I started the training. After the horse was saddled and bridled I mounted. Then the trouble started. Nothing in the world would induce the big black to leave the other horses and go out onto the road. I gave him the spurs, now without rowels but still good persuaders, and pulled his head around until his nose touched my toe. All he did was dance in a circle the other way. Doc tried leading him by the bridle. Doc was big, raw-boned and strong but not strong enough for the black. Then Doc tried the blindfold. If I had known the story of the previous attempt I would I think have said no. But I had not heard the story and was led like a lamb to the slaughter.

With an oat-bag over his eyes and me on his back the horse was led easily by Doc, holding the rein near the bit. The horse shivered a bit but made no protest. Down the road we went for a couple of hundred yards. The oat-bag was removed, I jabbed hard with my spurs and we were on our way. It was a lovely spring afternoon. The sun was bright and the fields were full of flowers. I was sure that the battle was won. All the big black was thinking of was where there was another horse that he could go and stand beside. There was nothing on the road but ourselves, neither man nor beast, until after a couple of miles we came to the village of Marqueffles. That is hard to spell and harder to pronounce, and to me the place is absolutely repugnant.

Half-way through the village we met a battalion of infantry on the march. They had been out in reserve and were like all troops after a rest, clean and smart with spotless uniforms, glistening buttons and well-shined boots. They swung along with that easy World War I step that could, and often did, take them twenty miles in a day. Often I have seen battalions like that go by our battery into the trenches; and often on an active front I have seen them come back a week or two later, a mere handful of what had been twelve hundred men, smothered in mud, unshaven, not a button shining and with feet that looked like cakes of dirty dough; but still swinging along, the mere handful of them, with that easy step—the PBI, the poor bloody infantry.

That day, however, they had their innings. Up front was a horse, the only horse in the column. On the horse was their colonel. The big black turned as we met the head of the column and fell in behind the colonel. I must give the brute credit for recognizing the colonel's rank and observing propriety by falling in behind the colonel instead of pulling up beside him.

I did my best to get out of the parade. I pulled the horse's head around until his nose touched my boot again. All that did was to put him into some sort of ballet dance and interrupt the march. Busy as I was with other things, I do remember that the infantry seemed to be enjoying the proceedings. At length I did succeed in getting out of the line of march, across the ditch and onto the sidewalk. There the black put his rear end through a plate glass window. How one could expect to find a plate glass window in Marqueffles I do not know, but the big black found one.

Then I gave up. A man can but do his best and I had long passed the point where I could do anything more. I dismounted and tried to lead that so-and-so horse away. He had other ideas; he had set his heart on being with the colonel's horse and no tugging or pulling would deter him. I mounted again and fell in behind the colonel. Fortunately the battalion was headed in the direction of our horse lines and I rode those two miles back at the pace of the marching men.

It was the same spring day as when I had come out; there were the same flowers in the fields and the sun still shone but somehow it seemed a different world because of those infantry marching behind me. They were marching at ease, which gave them a certain leeway, but did not, strictly speaking, justify the liberties that they took with me. No one took any steps to control them and I am afraid the officers enjoyed the spectacle I made as much as the men. I remember some of the things that were shouted at me but I am not going to record them. For forty-odd years I have been trying to forget them.

At long last we came to our horse lines. There I dismounted again. The piquet lines were in full view and the air to the big black was no doubt full of the smell of horses. He followed docilely as I led him into our lines. The infantry, damn them, gave me a loud cheer. That attracted the attention of everyone on the horse lines and underlined the manner in which I had returned. Jinnie got the big black back in his gun team and it stayed there until the end of the war.

Not long afterwards there was another bunch of remounts and I got Minnie. That settled all my outrider problems. She was a lovely sleek bay. She neck-reined as if she could read your mind and she could turn around in a smaller space than any other horse I ever rode. Her gait was perfect. When you rode her first you would swear that on her you could sleep in the saddle, which as a matter of fact I did more than once as you will hear later. It was on Minnie that I danced in the saddle for miles and miles during the open warfare of the last Hundred Days that preceded the armistice.

Minnie had another talent that I did not discover until after the armistice. She could outrun and outjump any other horse in the battery. The armistice when it came posed a new problem for Command. Everyone expected to go home at once. I do not know the figures but there must have been several hundred thousand Canadian soldiers in England and France. Several hundred thousand soldiers cannot all go down to the docks at once and say, "I want to go home." Besides the Canadians there were from overseas Australians, New Zealanders, South Africans, Indians and Americans all clamouring to go home. And there were only those ships that the submarines had not sunk to carry us. We had to wait our turn for what little shipping was available.

What does one do with an army out of work and waiting to be sent home? You cannot subject soldiers waiting for discharge to regular training. Even less can you let them sit idle with nothing to do but get into trouble. Soldiers have a sufficient aptitude for getting into trouble in their off hours even when they are kept busy. The problem was to keep us occupied with light and interesting things. Lack of occupation and delay in getting home to Canada led to the riots at Rhyl and Witley.

For the first two months after the armistice finding suitable occupation was no trouble in our battery. I have already told you that we were the training battery at Canadian Corps School at Habarque at the time when the armistice came. The school was continued and we had plenty to do supplying equipment until we were relieved in January. Then we moved forward to Grez-Doiceau about thirty miles southeast of Brussels. We were billeted in the village, had excellent stables and had nothing to do but look after the horses. You cannot groom horses all day, and to ask soldiers waiting for discharge to spend their time in foot drill would be to court the riots of Rhyl and Witley.

48

The answer to the problem in the artillery was exercise rides and mounted drill, fun on horseback. About eight miles to the west of us was the field of Waterloo, which was visited. About the same distance to the east of us was the scene of what Winston Churchill in his life of Marlborough called the Unfought Waterloo. It was a masterpiece of manoeuvre but as there was no battle it is not in the history books. None of us had heard of Ysche then, and it was not visited.

We did, however, have many wonderful rides over the Belgian countryside. Often when we came to open space with a ditch or two and a hedge we would have a race, a steeple-chase. Away we would go hell for leather over the meadows, the ditches and the hedges. Every time Minnie came in first. The first few times it was put down to accident or good luck but every race turned out the same way. If the war had not been over I am afraid that someone would have pulled rank on me and I would have lost Minnie.

Not long after that I said good-bye to Minnie. At the time I did not know that it was for good. I got leave to London and while there applied for a course at the Khaki College and did not return to Belgium. Often since I have wondered what became of her. I hope that she spent her last days in the stables and pastures of a good farm and not between the shafts of a *calèche* in Paris. I remember her soft lips as she nuzzled my hand or around my pockets for a bit of biscuit or chocolate. I hope she had lots of chocolate after I left her.

One cannot speak of army horses without thinking of the cavalry. Now and then one would talk to an old soldier who would say that in 1914 he had seen a cavalry charge. Sometimes a civilian would point to a plain near a village or wood and say that cavalry had charged there in the first months of the war. Occasionally we would see some troopers behind the lines, smart, well-turned-out men who looked like peacetime soldiers and who seemed to have nothing to do but ride their horses over the countryside. Now and then on a busy front someone would come into the lines telling us that he had seen the cavalry sharpening their sabres on big grindstones. That was always supposed to indicate that we were on the verge of a big break-through.

Only once did I see a cavalry charge. That was late in the war during the Hundred Days that finished it. Once I was nearly part of one, but that is another story. The charge I saw was on the second day of the great push in front of Amiens, the day after August eighth, which Ludendorf said was the blackest day of the war, when the Canadian Corps broke the Allied record for a single day's advance against an organized trench position.

On the second day, August ninth, we did something that we never did before, or afterwards for that matter, and that very few batteries ever did in World War I. We went into action in front of the infantry. We had spent the night in an open field near Demuin well behind the old German trenches. Then early in the morning we were on the march. Open warfare! We danced in our saddles and we danced in our saddles many days thereafter.

Presently we came to a wood not far from the village of Beaucourt. Behind the wood was something we had never seen before, a large body of cavalry, dismounted, the troopers standing at their horses' heads. We passed on and came to the corner of the wood where we paused. Then we started again, this time at a gallop. About the centre of the wood we got the order *Halt, action right!* We unlimbered and put our guns in action. The forward elements of the infantry were in the edge of the wood behind us. When they overcame their astonishment at seeing us in front of them they came out of the wood with their tin hats on the ends of their bayonets and gave us a cheer. That cheer was no doubt partly for themselves and to let off steam. They were as sure as we were that things were going very well. They were out of the trenches at last. In one day they had broken and penetrated a complete defensive position, and were in the open. They were as happy as we were. They had no horses to ride, nor saddles to dance

50

in, but like us they had begun to feel that the shores of Canada were not far over the horizon.

Shortly after that the cavalry came by. We had come around the right side of the wood; the cavalry came around the left side at a brisk trot, with jingling accoutrements and making a brave show. As they approached the village they broke into a gallop and disappeared into the shade trees on the outskirts of the town. After a long time they came back at a brisk trot, with jingling accoutrements and making a brave show, but with many, many led horses. The led horses had empty saddles. We wondered at the time why more horses than men had come back. A cavalry charge, we thought, would have more horse than man casualties. It was only recently that I found the explanation. In the volume of *The Times History of the War* that covers Amiens I found that the Canadian cavalry "with great gallantry" had taken Beaucourt, dismounting when they reached the suburbs and cleaning out the cellars and strong points with small-arms.

As anti-climax it must be reported that after galloping up into action in the open in front of the infantry we did not fire a shot. And it must also be reported that in all that heroic setting one of our guns went into action without any ammunition. Someone at the horse lines had goofed. The loaded wagon that should have come up with the gun was sent to the ammunition dump to be filled and an empty wagon came up with the horses to move forward with the gun. It was my gun but not, for once, my error. There I was in the open in front of the infantry with a gun and no shells. That was soon rectified; shells were carried from each of the other wagons and in a few minutes we were ready for the order to fire that never came.

After we received the order to stand down we investigated something we had noticed as we came into position along the front of the wood. What we had seen was a patch about an acre in extent or more, where from a short distance you could not see the grass for dead Germans. We talked to the infantry in the wood and found out what had happened. We were told that the night before, just at dusk, the Germans had counter-attacked in close formation in an attempt to retake the wood. In the wood with the infantry were two tanks. If we had known that when we galloped into action in the open we would have felt much better. The tanks had stayed hidden in the edge of the wood withholding fire until the Germans were too close to retreat. What happened is best described by repeating an earlier phrase: you could not see the grass for dead Germans.

We walked among them looking for souvenirs but the infantry had had the first pick. There were no watches or money left. We had to be satisfied with shoulder straps and uniform buttons. The field was covered with poppies most of them in bloom, but some of them had already gone to seed. I picked some of the dry pods and sifted the seeds into an envelope that I used for my next letter home. It seemed to me that a bed of poppies would be a good souvenir of that spot and that day. Unfortunately when my mother received the letter she was so happy that when she opened it she did not notice the seeds, and by the time she read the part of the letter that mentioned them they were scattered and completely lost.

A few years ago I was back and found the place. The field where the dead Germans had lain was planted partly with potatoes and partly with barley. The barley was full of poppies. I filled an aspirin bottle with dry poppyheads and dug out three small potatoes to bring home for seed.

The army was a hotbed for rumours. It could hardly be otherwise. So seldom did we see newspapers that it was natural that most of what we knew of things going on outside our lines came to us in the form of gossip brought into the lines by transport drivers, or gleaned by our signallers over the line to Brigade. Many of our rumours were about places we were going to go. Salonika was one of the favourites. It popped up regularly and we spent many an evening around our braziers, hunting cooties and discussing the advantages, or otherwise, of such a move. Sometimes we were about to go to Italy. No one, so far as I recall, ever suggested the Dardanelles. Perhaps our rumours of moves were inspired by some idea of what could be considered an improvement; the Dardanelles could not have qualified for that.

Sceptical as we had become of rumours there was one time when we fell for them in a big way. We were feeling wonderful at the time and were ready to believe anything. It was the second day of the Hundred Days. We were in the spot in front of the infantry where we saw cavalry in action. By the time we got the order to stand down the signallers were getting "news" over the brigade wire. I have often wondered how the rumours originated. Perhaps someone in charge of morale started them, though certainly at that time we needed nothing to boost our morale. We had done very well and were aware of it.

First of all came the "news" that the day before, while we had been crashing through, the British had attacked at Ypres, retaking Passchendaele, and had a bag of eighteen thousand prisoners and eight hundred guns. We had hardly digested that when the story came through that the French had broken the line on the *Chemin des Dames* front and had captured fifteen thousand prisoners and seven hundred guns. That was not all. Shortly after that we heard that the Americans, too, had struck, breaking the line on a wide front with a bag equal to the French, fifteen thousand prisoners and seven hundred guns. Seldom have I been so excited. We gathered around a map and tried to assess the news. Four clean breaks! The whole front in flames! We started making calculations. At eight miles a day, which was peanuts after what we had done the day before, we would be in Berlin long before Christmas, even allowing for some delay in getting over the Rhine. Whoever started those yarns deserves credit for something. He gave us some moments of rapture that we might otherwise never have experienced. Even the let-down, when we learned the truth, did not spoil that day of excitement. By then we were definitely on the move and knew fully that every step we took brought us closer to home.

5: Guns and Gunners

A sound of battle is in the land.
JEREMIAH 50:22

Although I was a gunner, and a limber-gunner and gun-layer at that, I have hardly said a word so far about guns. That must be corrected at once. My battery was a field battery equipped with eighteen-pounders. Our principal duty was the laying down of barrage, a curtain of fire made up of air-bursts of shrapnel placed in front of advancing infantry to disorganize the enemy and make them keep their heads down, or in front of our trenches to repel attack. We were also used for harassing fire, periodical shots at crossroads and communication trenches.

And of course we were used for targets of opportunity. One such target presented itself in the early summer of 1918 when we had our guns in Lieven on the Vimy front. It was a bright summer morning when we got the order to stand to. What follows was gleaned from the signallers when they came down from the observation post. The German front line was at the bottom of a small slope, really a long gentle rise. Connecting the front-line trench with the support trench at the top of the crest was a zigzagging communication trench. A German soldier passing through that trench had a sudden call of nature and climbed out into the open to respond to the call. We got our first shell between him and the trench about the time that he got his field-grey trousers down. Instead of ducking back into the communication trench he ran away from the shellburst and across the open fields toward the reserve trench at the top of the crest. We kept after him dropping shells just behind him and never quite catching up with him. At last he disappeared into the reserve trench. Up to the time that he disappeared he had not managed to get his pants up.

It was seldom that we knew what we were firing at or had any idea of the results obtained. I personally fired many thousands of rounds but have no reason to believe that I ever hit anything. Never, I am happy to say, did we use open sights. That would have meant firing at advancing Germans who had already passed our infantry and was something that was not included in our ambitions. Much of our work was night firing. I think of one such harassing job at the Somme. One special chore there was to fire two hundred rounds a night at some selected target, probably a communication trench. The task was divided into four parts—we were four-gun batteries at first—and each gun fired fifty rounds spread over a quarter of the night.

Number one gun crew fired first and when they were done they woke up the crew of number two gun, which fired its quota and then woke up number three and so on. You ask what I mean by waking gunners in a firing battery. I will astonish you further by saying that not only did the gunners in the other crews sleep while a gun was being fired but that all but one of the gunners in the crew of the firing gun slept during the firing of that harassing shoot. The first time I saw a gunner asleep beside a firing gun I thought it was a fake. I soon found out that it was a fact by doing it myself. A tired gunner could, and often did, sleep beside or even under a firing field gun.

Before the night firing had gone on very long it was realized that with the slow rate of fire one man could handle the gun by himself. The arrangement was simple. Before we rolled up in our blankets for the night the man who was to do the firing on the next gun came in and was told who would do the firing for us and was shown the spot where he would sleep. Then our duty man visited the gun-pit that was to follow us and obtained similar information. Under that arrangement two hundred rounds were fired every night by four men and not another man was roused.

My place to sleep in that gun-pit was on the left of the trail with my head near the spade and my feet under the gun-layer's seat. An eighteen-pounder had a recoil of forty-one inches. At the end of the recoil the breech of the gun was directly over my head and not more than a foot and a half away from it. Often in the morning after night firing I found grease, spit from the breech, in my whiskers. Never once did I wake up.

Only once was any other member of the crew roused. That was one night when I did the firing. The routine of firing was quite simple. We had fixed ammunition and the propellant charge was in a brass shell case attached to the shell. The night I had trouble the shell slipped from my hand as I was preparing to reload. It landed, the whole eighteen pounds of it plus the cartridge case and charge, on our sergeant's instep. He did what a firing gun could not do and woke up the whole gun crew. It was very much like the night in camp in Canada when a latecomer returning from a midnight pass was unable to resist a sudden drunken impulse and woke the whole bunkhouse when he put a tablespoonful of raspberry jam in his sleeping bunkmate's ear.

When we moved into that position new gun-pits were constructed by a working party from our horse lines, reinforced by members of the brigade ammunition column. The men of the column got a chance to work on everybody's dirty chores. In due course our guns were in place and laid on their proper night lines and we were ready for action again. Then we settled down.

A new gun-pit was a most unhomelike thing at any time. It consisted of a hole in the ground and a roof of planks or sheet metal covered, if we were lucky, with sandbags. There was a hole in the front for the gun muzzle and another hole at the rear, usually covered by a rubber groundsheet, for the crew to get in and out. For furnishings there were piles of ammunition. The gunners could sleep anywhere on the floor

56

that we could unroll our blankets. The rain had come down in cold sheets all the time we were moving and continued through the night. We were all cold and wet.

We got a fire going, using an old oil drum with holes punched in its sides for a brazier. As all our fuel was wet it generated much more smoke than heat, but we managed to keep the smart from our eyes by lying on the dirt floor with our heads below the haze of acrid fumes that filled the gun-pit. From time to time someone had to go out into the rain to find more fuel. When it was my turn to go I found four men sleeping in improvised lean-to's outside the gun-pit. Each of them had set two bits of scantling against the side of the gun-pit and then covered them with empty sandbags. That had the effect of breaking the direct beat of the rain and channelling it into dribbles that by skilful manoeuvring could be avoided, sometimes. The men were members of the working party from the ammunition column who had helped to build the gun-pits. Of course I asked them to come in and share our comfort. Soon we were all rearranged on our backs with our heads below the smoke.

Presently one of our guests spoke to one of the others. "How about a song, Mac?" he said.

It turned out that the real name of the man addressed as Mac was Skean and that MacDonald was his stage name. He was a tenor and had sung the leads in a number of Broadway musical shows. Some years before the war he had had throat trouble and then had done some producing, including a road edition of *Pretty Mrs. Smith* for Oliver Morosco. I had seen and heard him in Toronto where he had been one of a quartette appearing at Shea's on Victoria Street. Like many Americans he had come up to Canada to enlist while Uncle Sam was still neutral and had landed in France to do chores with the ammunition column. For two or three nights while the working party was still with us we lay on our backs in the reeking gun-pit and listened to light opera sung by a top-flight professional. Shortly after that we heard that Mac had gone to the Fourth Division concert party where he spent the

57

rest of the war behind the lines entertaining troops out on rest.

Just before the Vimy show we had a lot of bad ammunition. A large percentage of our time-fuses were defective. With one of the bad fuses the shell burst at the muzzle of the gun instead of over the target. That meant that the air in front of the gun was filled with a pint or so of shrapnel bullets about the size of small marbles, travelling at the speed of the muzzle velocity of the gun plus the momentum provided by the burst. In that cloud of lead there were also the big brass fuse that had malfunctioned to cause the premature, and the shell case. The shell case was intact; a shrapnel burst was like the discharge of a small cannon, and the case had to be strong enough to contain the blast and direct all the bullets forward in a shower that, theoretically, would kill anything in an area twenty-five feet wide and one hundred feet long. We fired one round of battery fire with that ammunition some days before the push. That was one round from each gun at ten-second intervals. In the six rounds there were two prematures, one of which killed a Canadian officer and sergeant on the Arras-Souchez road a hundred yards or so in front of us.

We ourselves were in a very unpleasant position. We were in the front row of seven lines of guns and there were six batteries behind us firing prematures at us. All day and all night the air above us was filled with the whine of shrapnel bullets from premature bursts and the howl of fuses and shell cases. The only real protection we built in that position was in the form of thick sandbag walls behind the guns to keep out our own shrapnel.

We had not been in that position very long when the Germans began to resent our presence. From their contour maps it was easy to decide where we were likely to be located. Flash and sound ranging added to their knowledge, and their observation balloons and aerial photographs put the finishing touches to the job. Then the counter-battery heavies went to work. It is amazing the amount of heavy fire that could be put into a battery position without doing very much damage. They annoyed us but did not hit anything of importance until the day before the push. Then on Easter Sunday — we took Vimy Ridge on Easter Monday — they hit the gun next to mine. The great cloud of black smoke that went up from the burning ammunition must have been a heartening sight to the German gunners. They knew then that they had our battery pinpointed. We knew it, too, and were rather unhappy about it.

Early next morning we were roused and told that this was it. Zero hour was six o'clock. We had our breakfast and prepared for action. All our watches were synchronized with Brigade, as they had been daily for some days. On the second, fifteen hundred guns spoke with one voice. From that moment until the rate of fire relaxed some hours later we could not even hear our own guns above the din. It must have been an appalling experience for the troops in the trenches opposite especially when a few seconds later the rain of lead fell on the parapets of their trenches. A captured German officer told one of our signallers that he had never seen anything like it in the whole war. I have heard, and I believe, that never before or after was there a barrage to equal the one we laid down at Vimy Ridge. Of those fifteen hundred guns a thousand were field guns bursting shrapnel every fifteen seconds on every ten yards of enemy trench. The other five hundred guns were heavies, with a much slower rate of fire, pounding strong points and German batteries.

Seated on the gun seat and looking forward I had a perfect view of the spectacular display that almost immediately spread itself across the sky line. First there were the star shells, or Very lights, which floated over No Man's Land and lit it up like noonday. Then there were the SOS signals. They were of all colours and shapes, each having a special message for troops behind the line. The sky was soon full of them, a fantastic fireworks display running along the line in both directions as far as the eye could reach. It was still quite dark. There was a pitch-black sky behind the display and it made a perfect backdrop for the show. Presently the smoke from the bursting shells drifted up into the glare of the Very lights giving us a vivid impression of the hell on earth in the German trenches beneath. After a little time the Very lights had all burned out and the SOS signals had faded away. With our infantry swarming into their trenches, their custodians were by then no doubt busy with other matters.

About that time we became busy with other matters ourselves. The counter-battery heavy that had pinpointed us the day before and hit one of our gun-pits went into action. Even if the display had not died down that would have taken our attention from the pyrotechnics up front. The first coal-box landed directly in line with our gun and some distance beyond our front aiming-post. The second was on the same line and landed between the two aiming-posts. The third one was half-way between our gun and the first aiming-post. Another lift of the same distance would have put the fourth shell right on top of our gun. We knew, however, that that would not happen. The Germans were methodical gunners. When they started to shoot a pattern they carried it out to the end without variation. That was something that helped often to get us safely out of a shelled position. After the first three rounds you could tell exactly where the next shell would land. This time he was shooting what we called a *sweep and walk*. On that pattern three rounds were fired on one line at increasing ranges. Then the line was shifted to the gunner's right and three more rounds were fired at the ranges of the first three. This was repeated until the gun had fired twelve rounds on four lines; then the pattern was repeated. Long before the fourth shell landed we knew exactly where it would be.

We knew that we were out of danger, practically. There was, however, always the chance that the gun-layer might become careless in levelling his bubble and overshoot. Fortunately for us that German gun-layer was perfection itself that morning. We were also lucky that the officer firing the German battery overlooked something. The day before we had been pinpointed and we should have been pinpointed again on that Easter Monday. Sunday had been bright, sunny and mild. Overnight the weather changed. There was a cold raw wind blowing straight toward the German battery and after the attack started there was snow. Before the day was over there was an inch of it. That change in atmospheric conditions was a handicap for the push but it was a godsend to us. There were several corrections to that pinpointing range that should have been made to allow for atmospheric change and the strong headwind and which, in the excitement of the attack, were apparently overlooked. If they had not been overlooked that German heavy would have been ploughing up our gun-pits for an hour or so that morning instead of ploughing up the area of our aiming-posts.

Before we went to France we had a trip to Lark Hill, near Salisbury Plain, for firing practice. All of our training so far had been without live ammunition, and a gunner of course is not a gunner until he has fired his gun. It may seem strange, but my nerves were tenser the first time we fired our gun with live ammunition than when we first went into action in France. The first day at Lark Hill we fired indirectly from a concealed position. The second day we went into action on the top of a small hill and were told to use open sights. We thought that the army had gone to a great deal of trouble to make things realistic for us. The target we were given was a cute little cottage in the valley before us surrounded by a rose garden in full bloom. On the order to load we filled our gun breeches with shrapnel shells from our gun limbers. Then one of our officers said quite casually, "You aren't loaded with live shells, I hope?" That's exactly what we were loaded with, all four guns. No one had told us that we were just having drill that morning while one of the other batteries was on the range. That quaint little cottage in the valley was a real cottage and the roses in the garden were real roses. With open sights we could hardly have missed that target. We would certainly have hit the garden at least.

I have mentioned a gun being hit and perhaps the reader is wondering how often that happened. The answer is that it did not happen very often in spite of the efforts that were made to do it. We had some nasty hits and more than once a whole gun crew was knocked out but on the whole we were very lucky. One exception was Passchendaele. We had more guns knocked out there in six weeks than we had in all of the rest of the war.

I find it hard to write about Passchendaele. Whenever I think of it my gorge rises. In starting these pages I put a restriction on myself not to say anything bitter. After more than forty years why should one be bitter? Passchendaele refuses to conform to that resolution. It is hard not to be bitter when one thinks of the priceless and irreplaceable assets that could have been used to so much better advantage, such as reinforcements for Byng in front of Cambrai or a drive in front of Vimy, which were frittered away to complete an unprofitable campaign so that Command could say that objectives had been reached. I know that I can add nothing to what has been said so many times but, as one who will never forget the hell it was, I feel that Passchendaele confirms the statement, made by someone whose name I have forgotten, that war is much too important a matter to be entrusted to generals. I feel like the old Frenchman I talked to in Paris while on leave after the facts of Passchendaele had begun to be known. He sat at a table in a *boulevard* café with tears running down his cheeks, sipping his wine and moaning, "Oh, dose English general. Oh, dose English general."

That opinion was not limited to Frenchmen. I find this in the *Encyclopedia Britannica,* which usually is as emotional as a dead codfish:

The curtain was at last rung down on the pitiful tragedy of 'Third Ypres.' It was the long overdue close of a campaign which had brought the British armies to the verge of exhaustion, one in which had been enacted the most doleful scenes in their history, and for which the only justification evoked the reply that, in order to absorb the enemies' attention and forces, the Higher Command had chosen the spot most difficult for the defender and least vital to the attacker.

The Canadian Corps was taken from positions we had prepared for a new push in front of Vimy and put into Passchendaele in October to polish off a summer of murderous and profitless fighting by taking Passchendaele village and ridge. The theory was that with the high ground taken the Germans would have to fall back from the whole Belgian coast. The "ridge" was about as high as a billiard table and when it was taken the Germans just sat back and pounded us on it. To take it we had only to advance about a mile and a half on a three-mile front. That looked simple to the men back at headquarters who, according to Lloyd George, never did appreciate the nature of the terrain until they saw it long after the battle. The corps went in something less than seventy thousand strong. The ridge was taken, and held. It cost us more to hold it than to take it. The cost? Sixteen thousand casualties, more than four thousand for every square mile taken and held.

We had our usual six guns in action there. By the time we came out we had had twenty-three guns knocked out. They were not all destroyed and some of them were back in action again in a few days. We worked with skeleton gun crews. Our duties were limited pretty much to barrage work. A gun crew consisted of an NCO and two or three men instead of the usual six. Our average strength at the gun lines including officers, signallers and the cook was thirty-six. From among these we had sixty-three casualties, of whom fifteen were killed. I spent thirty-one months in France and Belgium and I would do all of the rest of it over again rather than those six weeks at Passchendaele.

At the time we were not bitter. We knew very well that you cannot win wars without fighting. We thought that we were doing something very useful. It was only when we learned later of the futility, yes, and the fatuity of it, that we became bitter.

At our second position there we had bivies close to the guns. They were soon spotted and shelled heavily causing serious casualties. The guns could not be moved from their position by the plank road but new bivies were built a little to a flank. There they were soon seen by the hawk-eyes opposite. Notice of that fact was served on us in the form of a brisk bombardment. Our new bivies were in bad ground and were the original two-man affairs, with a roof that you touched with your shoulder if you rolled over. Sweating it out in my bivy with my bunkmate, the acting sergeant-major, we were discussing the advisability of moving our quarters again. That presented problems. There was very little land convenient to the guns on which a bivy could be built. Even if we could move it would be very little help, for the SOBs would find us again on the first clear day. Passchendaele was one place where we loved fog and mist.

Presently there was a howl that told our experienced ears that something was coming and that it was going to land very near to us. That is exactly what it did, but without an explosion. There was an earth-shaking thud, which threw me clear of the ground. Almost before I landed back on my duckboard my companion was curled around me, trying to find a spot where he could tilt the rum jar, in his custody as sergeant-major, to take a swig. After we each had a drink we went outside to see what had happened. There we found that a howitzer shell had cut away half of the sandbag against which my shoulder had been resting, without exploding, and had disappeared into the mud beneath our bivy. We went inside and had another drink. If that shell had been properly made and its fuse had operated as it should have, four feet or so below the surface, there would no doubt be small pieces of me and the acting sergeant-major still floating in the stratosphere over Belgium.

64

The mud of Passchendaele was in some ways a good thing. Many shells were smothered by it when they burst and there was not nearly the danger from splinters flying great distances, which we often experienced on other fronts. Some shells, particularly small ones, were completely smothered. One of my friends was standing by his bivy one day when a percussion whiz-bang landed directly under him. He rose in the air on a cushion of mud and landed on the other side of his bivy. He got up unhurt, scraped away what mud would come off easily and shook his fist eastward, demanding of those SOBs what the hell they thought they were doing. Psychologically, a little profanity was a great relief. One of our boys lost an arm in Vimy village. The men who took him away reported how he went back over the ridge, shaking his remaining fist at the Germans and cursing them in language, which, when reported to us, was the wonder and admiration of the whole battery.

One day in Passchendaele we had a taste of those rubber-heeled babies, the kind that came faster than sound and that you heard approaching after they burst. Rumour had it that the gun was a twelve-inch railway gun. If you told me that it was a twenty-inch gun I would not argue with you. Only three shells from it came into our area. The first landed about one hundred yards ahead of us. Having no warning I was standing facing it when it landed, sending a volcano of mud and water into the air. The concussion from that shellburst one hundred yards away felt exactly as if someone had hit me in the stomach with a plank. My greatcoat, as always there, was soaked and caked with mud. The skirt of it flew out parallel with the ground. Long before the second shell came over I was away on a flank. The second shell landed squarely on our line of guns. From where I was it seemed that two of our guns had been hit. It looked very much as if that big gun was being fired by someone with an accurate means of observation. The third shell dispelled that idea. It landed one hundred yards to the rear of our guns. There were only three shells at intervals of one hundred yards in an area that was crowded with guns, fired apparently at the area generally, with the hope that one at least would hit something.

When we were sure that it was all over we returned to our guns. Nothing had been hit, though two of our guns had been missed by inches only. The shell hole was at least twelve feet deep and thirty feet across. The lip of the shell hole was within a couple of feet of the trail of one of our guns. On the seat of that gun when the shell burst was its limber-gunner. As the first shell was a hundred yards away he had decided to sweat it out. Before the third one landed he was with us on the flank, still pretty short of breath. If that shell had landed ten feet shorter, he and both guns would have been on the casualty list.

Sometimes splinters did fly at Passchendaele. I was hit by two of them without getting even a Blighty. One day, when we had been shelled out, I was sitting with my back against a German pillbox, when a long shiny piece of shell, about eight inches long, two inches thick and two inches wide settled in the crook of my arm and stayed there. It did not even sting. It had come several hundred yards and I would guess that it must have hit the roof of the pillbox and bounded from there onto my arm. The other piece that hit me was about the same size; it was not bright and shining, but black and partly rusted. It hit me on the ankle and did not penetrate the leather of my knee boots, but it did break the surface of the skin beneath. For several days I walked with a decided limp. I have often wished that I had had sense enough to keep one or both of those shards as souvenirs. At Passchendaele we were not thinking of souvenirs; all we wanted in that line was our hands and feet.

Bursting shells did not always break evenly. One side of a shell might split into big ugly shards and the rest of the shell might disintegrate into a shower of needle-like splinters. Even tiny splinters could do great damage. A small splinter hit one of our gunners at Vimy, penetrating his shrapnel helmet in front, passing completely through his skull and out through the tin hat behind. That one was not a Blighty. We

66

gave our tin hats rather querulous glances after that. One of our signallers got a tiny splinter through the lower part of his temple at Passchendaele, so small that when the wound healed there was no scar either at the point of entry or exit. It was not too small, however, to destroy the optical nerve and leave him totally blind. In Vimy village two of our gunners on guard were standing shoulder to shoulder chatting. A big shell landed just behind them. One of the men was killed. They told us at the dressing station that he was practically flayed, his back riddled by tiny splinters. The other man did not have a scratch.

The worst bombardment I was ever in was on the fourteenth day of November, 1917, at Passchendaele. I will explain later why I am so sure of the date. In spite of the mauling we had received and the difficulties under which we had worked, the field artillery had done a good job. Not only had we fired the barrage that made the capture of the village possible, but we had helped to repulse some counterattacks and had done much to harass communications. The time had come when we were to be eliminated The way we were grouped, almost hub to hub, around the plank-road was practically an invitation to a counter-battery commander. The first shells landed at twelve noon. They were in the form of a gigantic many-battery salvo that blanketed our whole gun area. A few minutes later, when I had reached a flank, I made a count. Those big 5.9s were coming at the rate of twenty per minute. All heavies on that part of the front must have been concentrated to celebrate my birthday. That is why I remember the date. They kept it up at approximately that rate until five minutes after five. Why they ran over the even five hours I can only guess. Perhaps some of the guns moved in for the shoot were told to fire away the rest of their ammunition before they moved back to their regular positions.

It was a sight to see, especially from a safe flank. The whole gun area was covered by a billowing pall of black smoke, pierced in places by new bursts and the flames of burning ammunition. It was hard to believe that anything could come unhit through what we saw. When we went back it was to an area of wrecked bivies, smashed and upturned guns and charred ammunition piles. The amazing thing was that so much had survived. A lot of us had to build new bivies that night and those who did slept without blankets. Every November fourteenth since then, except one, I have had a telephone call or letter from the corporal who had spent most of that afternoon with me on the flank. On the one occasion when he did not call or write, I had a phone call from his wife. "Fred," she said, "had his appendix out this morning. Before he went into the operating room he asked me to phone you and wish you many happy returns and remind you of Passchendaele."

A few days later we had an encore. It was not nearly so heavy and did not last so long. It was concentrated more on the plank-road. After we got to the flank a gunner came along who said that a man had been hit and needed help. We expressed sympathy. "You're Thirtieth, aren't you?" he asked. I admitted it. "Well," he said, "it is one of your men." Then he kept going to the flank.

We got a stretcher party together and located a stretcher. Back near the plank-road we found our man. He was in a bad way. He had been hit in the throat and was bleeding freely. The cardigan jacket he wore was so covered with blood that you could not see the seams of the garment. None of us knew what to do in a case like that so we put him on the stretcher and started for the dressing station. We were a little distance from the plank-road and most of the shelling was there so we went overland to the dressing station. It was I think about half a mile but it may have been a little over a quarter of a mile. At every step we went knee-deep in mud. We should have gone to the plank-road, for the short cut we took was across land somewhat lower than the gun position and was little better than a swamp. As we struggled through

68

trying to make time, with a comrade on our shoulders bleeding to death, we were nearly frantic. As soon as we delivered our burden to the doctor I opened my tunic and stripped off my gas mask in an attempt to get my breath back. In places like that we always wore our gas masks at the alert, just under our chins. Mine was completely soaked with perspiration from my face. It would hardly have been wetter if it had been dipped in a pail of water.

The doctor put some iodine on a bit of cotton and placed it in the wound. Then he covered the body with a blanket and had the stretcher placed in a waiting ambulance. One of our boys crawled into the ambulance to speak to the wounded man. His hands came out from under the blanket with a thumbs-up gesture. That is the story we took back to the battery; thumbs up and doing fine. I wonder that we could have been so stupid. We had seen that terrible gash in the throat and the blood-caked cardigan and we had seen the doctor put him in the ambulance with no attention but a bit of gauze in the wound. We should have known better. He was dead long before the ambulance stopped at the cemetery outside Ypres.

Two of our party of four carrying the stretcher are still at Passchendaele.

For a while in 1918 I had charge of an anti-tank gun in the front-line trenches. That was shortly after the Germans made their great break-through on March twenty-first. In that offensive the Germans had used tanks for the first time, I think. It was only then, I know, that we did anything about a special tank defence.

We were out of line for a few days near Lens. One morning on nine o'clock parade the major told us that our brigade had been ordered to man an anti-tank gun. He did not say anything about the front-line trenches. He did tell us though that our battery had been assigned the duty and he wanted volunteers. I now had my third stripe but was spare sergeant and had not yet got my gun. First, the major said, he needed an NCO. Naturally he looked straight at the spare sergeant. I remembered the corporal with his "I want one volunteer. Happy, you go," and stepped forward. Soon we had a full gun crew.

Fortunately we did not have to put the gun in position. The engineers performed that task for us and all we had to do was go up and take over. What we took over startled us. It was a museum piece. We had been trained to use and had been using an up-to-date gun with a traverse of four degrees each way. That is, we could move the gun in an arc of eight degrees by turning a wheel and without moving the trail. This South African veteran had a total traverse of one degree. To change line out of that one degree arc we had to release the brakes, lift the spade at the end of the trail and turn the piece with the gunners heaving on the gunwheels and the number one, meaning the NCO in charge, breaking his back struggling with the trail handle. Then we had to re-set the brakes and get the tank in our open sight provided it was still in our one degree arc. Quite obviously both gun and gun crew were considered by someone at headquarters as being expendable.

Our standing orders modified that a bit: *In case of attack with tanks, destroy all tanks, destroy the piece and retire.* The gun was clearly expendable and we were, too, until such time as we had destroyed all tanks, provided that the German infantry had not already reached us. I used to hope that the tanks, if they came, would be obliging enough to keep within that one-degree arc.

The gun-pit was built into the parapeted east side of the trench with an opening in front for the gun muzzle and for observation. The opening in daylight was covered by a fish-net camouflage, a coarse netting with patches and strips of canvas on it, to conceal the gap in the parapet. The first night we were there, like good gunners we rolled up in our blankets around the gun on the gun-pit floor. Shortly after dark something happened that changed our sleeping habits completely. We were just comfortably rolled up in our blankets and getting ready to drop off when a German machine-gunner across No Man's Land caught the parapet of our trench with a sudden burst of harassing fire. Our pit opening was in the face of the parapet, and a dozen or so machine-gun bullets came popping in the opening, ricocheting around off the gun and ammunition. You never saw six gunners move so fast in your life. In nothing flat we were out of the gun-pit and around the corner of the trench draped with trailing blankets that we had not bothered to remove. That night we slept in the trench. Before the next night came we had dug ourselves a shelter in the side of the trench.

It was a quiet life. No tanks came over. Each morning, an hour before dawn, we rose and manned the gun and waited for them. After breakfast we had an hour or so of gun drill, getting so that we handled that clumsy old relic as I am sure it was never handled before. It is amazing what enthusiasm can be put into gun drill if you may have to use your skill with the coming of the next dawn. The rest of the time we spent mostly playing poker. I never had such a run of cards in my life. For the month we were there, playing eight or ten hours a day, I never got up fom the game a loser. In no time at all I had all the money in the gun crew. After that the boys paid off with IOUs and I collected such a prodigious pile of them that all of us knew that they were impossible to redeem. As a tribute to the good sense of my gunners I must record that none of them ever attempted the impossible. All troops love to gamble when they have anything with which to gamble. No one could quarrel with that. Every day we took the greatest gamble a man can take and often the odds were not favourable. Every two weeks, unless we were on an active front, we were paid the equivalent of three dollars. Then the gambling began. Some preferred poker, most of us played crown and anchor. None of us played craps until the Americans arrived, and not many even after that. When we had no money we played five hundred. A few highbrows played auction bridge. The odds at crown and anchor

71

were we knew against us, but we loved the action and we were used to unfair odds. One of our men operated a board regularly and got all our pay. He was an engineering graduate and had some pals with the engineers. When their lines were near ours, after he had cleaned us out he went over to the engineers' officers' mess and played poker. I can only conclude that he was not a good poker player; all our money stayed with the engineers. When our lines were adjacent the liquor for that mess was bought with our pay.

Our colonel's groom used to operate a crown and anchor board at brigade headquarters. There he did a land-office business. Not only did he have the headquarters staff to work on but all of the crown and anchor magnates from the batteries were his customers. They should have known better. They knew that the odds were all in favour of the board and yet, after proving that by taking our money, they went to the brigade board and left our money there. One day the colonel's horse kicked the groom and broke a couple of his ribs. The adjutant volunteered to get his kit for him before he left for the hospital. One kit-bag puzzled the adjutant. It was one of the long round ones, usually called duffel bags, shaped like a section of sewer pipe, about a yard long and nearly a foot thick. It had an odd feel and the adjutant succumbed to his curiosity and opened it. It was filled with paper money, over twenty thousand francs in fact, more than four thousand dollars. The colonel immediately forbade the playing of crown and anchor in the brigade lines. That only made it more popular than ever.

Once, after I was relieved from my anti-tank gun I had a ride in a tank. I was at the horse lines near Aix-Noullette for some time and there one morning I was in charge of a party grazing horses. In the plain near our grazing horses were some tanks practising crossing a sunken road some fifteen or twenty feet deep. After I had been watching them for some time a young tank officer came to where I was standing. "Would you like a ride, Canada?" he said—*Canada*, not

72

sergeant. From an Imperial that was breath-taking. Naturally I said, "Yes, sir."

A tank was halted and a port at the side was opened for me to enter. While I was getting in a mechanic opened a five-gallon drum of oil and took some out for his motor. Away we went down the bank into the road, with me holding onto the machine-gun at my side to keep from rolling down to the front of the tank. We crossed the road and started up the other side. The tank seemed to stand on end, and I kept from rolling to the back by hanging on again to the machine-gun. The can of oil had nothing to hang onto as we climbed and started to roll. It was not until it came to rest squarely in my lap that I noticed that the mechanic had forgotten to replace the cap after he had withdrawn his bit of oil. By the time we were on level ground again I had between two and three gallons of heavy machine oil all over my smart Bedford cord breeches.

If entertaining the troops were a meritorious service I should have had some sort of citation. Everyone in the battery except the sergeant-major seemed to think my breeches were funny. The SM regarded me with a fishy eye and said, "That's what you get when you put stripes on some people."

While I was having my time with my anti-tank gun one of our bombardiers was leading a life of fraud and deception a mile or so behind me. In an open field with a little crest, but really not enough to be good flash-cover, six mounds were built to resemble gun-pits. Logs of wood were placed in front to look like gun muzzles. From the air it must have looked exactly like a badly camouflaged battery. My friend was put in charge as OC Dummy Battery. He was given a large supply of "ammunition" that, when ignited by a short fuse, went off with a quick bright flash, which from the other side of the crest must have looked exactly like a gun flash. When any of our batteries were firing at night Dinny would fire his fake flashes. Counter-battery spotters in the opposite lines would see those bright flashes and ignore the dull glow of the well-crested real batteries. By sighting from the base of a triangle of which the dummy battery was apex, the position of that battery was easily calculated. The cost of the heavy ammunition fired by the Germans into that empty field would probably have built a squadron of tanks.

One of our officers did a nice piece of shooting at Wallers, the last place we fired our guns. The officer at our observation post was a recent replacement, a dashing, gay-hearted Irishman, who later had an excellent World War II record to add to his earlier experiences. Up the road from the observation post, which was in the railway station and with the first line of infantry, was a farmhouse with a stone dairy attached. In the dairy were a couple of enemy machine-guns that swept the road and made further advance a bothersome operation. The railway station of course was well marked on the map but the dairy was not. Even in daylight it would have been hard to estimate the exact distance and it would have had to be destroyed by directed fire. But this was night and the infantry were supposed to push on just before dawn. It was a matter of life and death for some of those infantrymen that those two machine-guns be eliminated before dawn.

The officer crawled up the ditch by the side of the road on his belly measuring the distance as he went and then sat with his back against that dairy full of Germans to make a note of the figures in case he should forget them on the way back. That was our last target of the war and we had a lovely shoot. We slept on the stone floor of what was left of the dairy the next night and we were very proud of the fact that we had made several solid hits on it and had fouled our next night's nest. The officer took it all in his stride. We would never have heard of it if it had not been for the signallers.

Ranging the guns was a frequent chore. Every time we moved our guns they had to be fired in. Our position would be located mathematically on the map, but maps are not always perfect and we had to register on the target area allotted to us. After a while, too, each gun had to be registered for range. Eighteen-pounders were designed for a life of one thousand rounds. By 1918 most of our guns had fired twenty thousand rounds and were still good for many more but they had naturally developed individual characteristics. Wear and tear on the gun barrels and the resulting loss of propellant gas made great differences in range. Eventually each gun had a table of allowances to be made to adjust to loss of muzzle velocity.

Our classic case of ranging was in Arras with guns near the railway station, in the last position we had before we went south to Amiens to join the great push that finished the war. The ranging was done with a gun of which I had temporary charge. After we were ordered to stand to we were given a line, a range and an elevation. When we were all set I reported, "Ready, sir," and we got the order to fire. Almost immediately we got the order to stop. That was superfluous as in ranging we only fired on order, but perhaps indicated that someone was upset by what had happened. We got the order to repeat, followed promptly by another unnecessary squawk to stop. There was a long pause and then I got the order to check. I was in charge but without an order I would not ordinarily check the instruments. I checked and found everything in order. I reported and we fired again. Then the captain came out of the command post and checked all the instruments himself. There was a long wait. At last we got a new line, a new range and a new elevation and registered in a few rounds. It was not until the signallers came down that we found out what had happened.

The officer who had conducted the ranging had in many ways done an excellent job. He had made only one mistake. He had figured line, range and elevation perfectly—to where he was instead of the target. We had put three rounds within twenty-five yards of the observation post and had very nearly blown him and the signallers off the map. As I said, it was a classic ranging.

6: Laugh or Go Mad

And if I laugh at any mortal thing,
   'Tis that I may not weep.
LORD BYRON

Seated in our gun-pit at the Somme in our first position on
the lip of the old Sugar Trench we saw two officers walking
along the sky line of the slight crest in front of us. The Germans saw them, too, and started after them with whizz-bangs,
shrapnel air bursts. The officers started to run. The shrapnel
followed them. The officers ducked into a shell hole and
shelling changed to HE ground bursts. The officers got out
of the shell hole and ran again, followed by more shrapnel.
Finally they got off the sky line and the shelling stopped.

What did we do? What could we do? We sat in our gun-pit
and howled with laughter. They were two Canadian officers,
perhaps from our home town, and certainly no one that we
had anything against. If we could have helped them there is
nothing that we would not have done. We could not do anything, so we laughed our heads off. Nothing could have
stopped our laughter except one of the officers being hit.
They were not hit, so we just laughed.

I have often wondered about that event. There was really
nothing funny about it. The Germans were trying to kill two
of our men and we laughed as if we were watching a funny
movie. Perhaps the word *movie* is the clue. The great comic
of those days and for long after was Charlie Chaplin. Some
critic has said that the basis of Chaplin's humour was the
sudden collapse of a great and overwhelming cardboard
dignity. That will bear consideration. Chaplin in his tawdry

76

clothes was a figure of great dignity. It was a cardboard dignity but it was there. You knew that he felt important and was consciously dignified. Then something went wrong. That was where the laugh came.

Certainly our officers had dignity. We recognized their position, stood at attention in their presence and addressed them as "sir," but we knew that that, in a sense, was due to a sort of fiction necessary to military discipline but no more real than the cardboard dignity of Charlie Chaplin. All of us can name many men who made great names for themselves after the war and who never held a commission. I can name offhand a judge of the Supreme Court of Canada, a financier who built up a great fortune, an outstanding public administrator. In our battery there were four men who never even had a stripe who became colonels in World War II. We all knew that the gulf between the ranks, though necessary, was arbitrary and in a sense a sham. The collapse of that cardboard dignity may have been the reason for our mirth.

That may be a partial explanation but I do not think that it goes to the root of the matter. At the Somme and at a good many other places we were under great emotional stress. That I need hardly explain. Emotional stress needs an outlet. I think that perhaps we laughed because we had to do something, and of course we could not cry.

We laughed a good deal. It seemed that whenever we were not grousing we were laughing. All soldiers, in peace as well as war, are grousers. And we groused a lot. A stranger in our lines unfamiliar with soldier psychology would have thought that we were on the verge of mutiny. I recall the story of the general who was curious about the morale of his men. It is an old story and has been told many times but it illustrates my point. He wandered after dark through the lines listening to the men in the tents or dug-outs and returned to his quarters well satisfied. "They are grousing," he said, "just as they did in England. Their morale is high."

By the grousing standard our morale was high. Most of the time we were grousing; the rest of the time we were laughing or perhaps singing. What times we had in the *estaminets* behind the lines and in the bathhouses. To hear a gang having a bath in one of those improvised bathhouses would have dispelled anyone's doubts about the army's morale.

Our songs were mostly army songs: "Mademoiselle from Armentières," "Keep Your Head Down, Fritzie Boy," "Carry Me Back to Blighty," "Pack Up Your Troubles in Your Old Kit-Bag," "Old McDonald Had a Farm," "Oh, Landlord Have You Cakes and Wine?" *Never* "Tipperary"; that was for folks at home. Some of the verses we sang were rather ribald. I remember Gitz Rice, who wrote "Mademoiselle," being introduced to the gang at one of the Corps reunions. "Yes," he admitted, "I wrote 'Mademoiselle from Armentières,' but I didn't write the verses you lugs sang." Certainly some of the verses we sang were pretty ripe. But for some reason we hardly ever had any smutty stories. An army in the field apparently does not generate such things. If we heard one it was brought to us by someone just back from leave or by a remount. Perhaps that stuff the Red Cross put in our drinking water had something to do with that.

Occasionally there was a different type of song. At a sing-song in a Salvation Army hut or tent someone would start, "There's a Long, Long Trail." I wish you could have heard us sing that. Unconsciously we put months and years of yearning into that song. It seemed to be an outlet for things that needed expression but could not be said. I could sing it then but I cannot sing it now. If I start it in the bathtub or on a long lonely motor trip, the only places I dare sing, I find that I cannot finish it. After more than forty years the emotions that that song expressed for me behind the lines in France rise up again and choke me.

Only twice in three and a half years in the army did I see tears. Once was on the troopship bringing us home. We were all on deck as we approached Halifax harbour. A great tear, the size of a pea, gathered in one of my eyes, rolled down to the end of my nose and splashed off onto the deck. My toughfibred little corporal was standing beside me and saw it. He looked at me in surprise and then smiled. It was not a derisive smile. I am emboldened to make this open confession by something I read in Arthur Bryant's *Triumph in the West*, based on Field Marshal Alanbrooke's diaries. He tells of an inspection made by Lord Alanbrooke and Winston Churchill at Tripoli. The Eighth Army had just completed twelve hundred miles of fighting along the north coast of Africa from El Alamein and were being rewarded by being allowed to polish up and march past the Prime Minister and Chief of the Imperial General Staff. In the march-past was the Fifty-First Division, the gallant old Highland Division, with swinging kilts and sunburned knees. The Field Marshal found a tear on one of his cheeks and, tough old soldier that he was, felt somewhat embarrassed and glanced quickly at Churchill to see if his weakness had been observed. He found tears on both the Prime Minister's cheeks.

There was one time in France when I wished that I could have cried. When I enlisted one of my best friends was in hospital undergoing an appendectomy. We had been students together in the same law office and were very close. After he got out of hospital he enlisted in a battery that had just been formed, and as I had joined an over-strength battery about to proceed overseas I got to France long before he did. After we took Vimy Ridge we heard that his division had landed in France. In July I got a few days away from the guns and went to look for him. His battery horse lines were only a mile or so from our horse lines so I walked over there the morning after I came down from Vimy village.

For months I had been looking forward to that moment. I asked for my friend and was told that he had been killed the night before in Vimy village, just about the time that I was leaving it. It was a hot July day and the news was almost more than I could take. The horse lines were near an old German trench. I went over and sat on the sandbag parapet. I was as near being physically sick as one can be without actually yielding. Part of it may have been out-of-the-line reaction, for we had been having a rough time of it in the village. After a while I got a drink of water from the battery water cart and walked back to our lines. That I think was my bitterest day in France. It was once when laughter could not have been a safety valve.

The other time I saw tears in the army was in the last Hundred Days. After we broke the first spur of the Hindenburg Line on September second we were out on rest for a few days. Rest in the army meant a change of activity and we spent the time practising open warfare. Then we went back in again in front of Cambrai for the push that went over the Canal du Nord and captured Bourlon Wood. The night before we went into the line again we were encamped in an open field, the guns and horses together. The cook-house was set up a few feet from the end of my piquet line. During evening stables I exercised my sergeant's prerogative and while the boys were cleaning the horses and mules walked over to the travelling kitchen to see what was coming up for supper and to have a mug of tea. One of my boys was on cook-house fatigue and was peeling potatoes. He was a jolly lad, all smiles no matter what came up. Presently the potatoes were all peeled and there was a bucketful of peelings to dispose of. About thirty feet away there was a patch of weeds and Ricky went to throw the peelings there. A moment later he was back, his face bathed in tears, and crying, unashamed, like a baby.

"Why, Rick," I said, "what's wrong?"

"Sarge," he sobbed, "I just found my brother's grave over there by the weeds."

And there it was, not thirty feet from our cook-house, a new grave with a rifle stuck into the soft earth to mark it and at the end of it a bit of board with the name and regimental number of Ricky's brother. They had not seen each other since they left Canada.

Although we sometimes laughed because some emotional outlet was necessary, some of the things we laughed at really were funny. There was the major in our brigade who was a casualty at Vimy Ridge. Peacetime equipment for artillery officers included a sabre. It was a very necessary part of a ceremonial salute. Some of the officers, including the major I am speaking of, had sabres with them in France. When the ridge was taken and we had to move forward into the village he buckled on his sabre to go over the ridge in style. His new quarters were in a deep German dug-out near the base of the ridge. Going down the stairs into the dug-out he tripped over his sabre, broke his leg and kept on rolling until he landed in Canada.

And then there was the officer who thought he had invented a flash-screen that would kill the telltale glow of the guns in action. We were in a reserve position on top of Vimy Ridge just behind the spot where the Vimy Memorial now stands. One morning on nine o'clock parade there was a call for the carpenters to fall out. Then, as usual, there was a call for the rough carpenters. In training that was a call that always had a big response, every man who could drive a nail without smashing his thumb claiming to be a rough carpenter to get out of foot drill. In an easy reserve position with nothing to do but eat and sleep there were not many rough carpenters, but the few who responded were enough for the job. Materials had been brought up from the rear and the men set to work. We paid little attention to them at first but as the work progressed we watched them with bug-eyed fascination.

First there was a scantling frame in the shape of a V that was covered with sheets of corrugated iron. We were so interested by this time that there were actually volunteers helping to carry those iron sheets from the spot where they had been piled when unloaded from the transport wagon. Finally the contraption was completed and the officer received permission to try it out. All of us except the crew of the gun firing were outside watching. A moment later there was a frantic scramble for cover. Practically every one of those metal sheets was torn loose by the concussion and went sailing into the air. The sheets on the top must have risen forty or fifty feet. Some of them sailed away like gliders. One went over the ridge. The Germans must have thought that an ammunition dump had blown up. No one ever bothered to gather up the sheet iron but the scantling made excellent kindling for the cook. That incident did much for our morale. But we all gave the officer a big A for effort.

When we could not laugh sometimes there was a crack-up. Battle fatigue was a common term in World War II. We called it shell-shock. A bad case of it was an unnerving thing to see. I remember well one I saw at Passchendaele, an infantryman, a mere boy, led by his comrades down the plank-road through our gun position to the dressing station. He was scarcely able to walk. His head and arms were shaking as if from convulsions. But there was no fear or horror in his eyes. Fear was not a necessary factor in shell-shock. One of the best men in our battery was shell-shocked at Vimy. That is hardly correct; he did not break up until he was back in hospital. He was full of guts and as long as there was any-thing he could do he kept control of himself. Only when there was no more need for him to hold on and when he relaxed did he break up.

Vimy village was full of guns. Day after day, after the ridge was taken, the Germans poured heavy shells into the village almost at random, knowing that a fair percentage of them would find a target. My gun crew slept in a wine cellar, a nice dry cellar with a vaulted brick roof and with several feet of broken bricks and rubble on top of it.

The sergeant in charge of our gun had a gramophone which, with a box of records, was carried carefully on the limber of our gun. We had them with us in that wine cellar. A popular song in England at that time was "Every Little While." We had a record of that. It soon acquired a bad name. Every time we put it on we were shelled. The superstitious blamed that on the record. The fact that we got shelled, too, if we did not put it on was considered to be beside the point. Some of the gang would get up and leave hurriedly every time it was played. Human nature being what it is, some of us made a point of putting that record on more than any of the others. I blush to admit that I was one.

One day the gun crew in the next cellar borrowed our gramophone. Our shell-shocked man was sergeant of that crew. Shortly afterwards someone came running to tell us that that cellar had been hit. We ran to see and help. We found that a large shell had hit the roof of the cellar near the stairs, blocking them and collapsing about half of the roof into the cellar. Willing hands soon dug a hole down the stairway large enough for one man to slip through. Two of the men in the cellar were buried under bricks. The other three had also been buried but had dug themselves free before we got there. John, the man I am talking about, was conducting them like a cheer-leader, "One, two, three—help!" It was that concerted cry that had brought help. A rope was lowered through the small hole that we had dug and the wounded men pulled out one at a time. I carried one corner of the stretcher on which the first man out went to the dressing station. When we got him there we were surprised to find that he was dead. There had been no haemorrhage and there were no apparent wounds. The MO told us that probably his heart had quit while he was buried under the bricks.

When I got back to the battery I heard the rest of the story. The gramophone had been at the end of the cellar that had not collapsed. It was playing "Every Little While" when the shell landed. It was still playing while John was digging his way out of the pile of bricks on top of him. The first thing he did when he got free was to stop the music. Then he organized and led the chorus for help. And he was the last man to go to the dressing station, on his own feet though badly bruised.

John was away for a long time and did not come back to us until we moved south for the Amiens push. There our horse lines were in a wood near Boves. The guns were in the open, so the gramophone was kept at the horse lines, in the sergeants' mess in a little hut built at the edge of the wood. The first night there after supper someone put on "Every Little While." It was not intentional, I swear; none of us had thought of the incident in Vimy village—except John. He turned deathly pale, got up and stood still a moment and then rushed to the door, which he barely reached. Outside he vomited violently. Without a word he went for a walk and did not come back for two or three hours. As soon as he had gone we broke that record. The incident was never mentioned by John nor by us in his presence. Courage, or lack of it, had nothing to do with shell-shock. I never knew a braver man than that long bony Highlander.

Few of us landed in France with any assurance that we could take what lay ahead. I believe that at first we were worried more about how we would take it than with what we would have to take. We welcomed our baptism of fire because it told us something that we were very anxious to know.

The first casualty we had in our brigade was a man who had to prove to himself that he could take it. His battery was under fire and everyone else took cover. He refused to move. He was sitting at the gun-pit entrance doing nothing, and there was no reason why he should not have stepped into the gun-pit where he would have been safe from anything but a direct hit. But he had to prove to himself that he was not afraid of gunfire or of being killed. Perhaps he was a bit elated, as most of us were in such a position, that the first few shells had not produced panic. Whatever his reason, he proved whatever it was he had to prove by getting the top of his head blown off. That was a useless and senseless casualty.

There were many like that among green troops. That is one of the reasons why seasoned troops, soldiers who have been blooded, are so much more effective than green troops. The old soldier knows the ropes and he knows how to give himself all the breaks it is possible to have. Before I had been in France three months I made the boast, which most of us were entitled to make, that I was never standing for any shell that landed within fifty feet of me and was never down for one that was more than one hundred yards away. It was uncanny how we could judge from the sound of an approaching shell exactly where it would land. Exception must be made of course of the high-velocity, rubber-heeled babies that came over occasionally from railway guns, travelling faster than the speed of sound. You heard them coming after they had burst. Towards the end of the war it was a treat to watch some old-timer who had to go through a heavily shelled area, a signaller, say, mending an important line, dodging from shell hole to shell hole, and using his knowledge of the pattern of the shoot that he had figured out before he started. The old soldier may not be as dashing as the new soldier but he is a lot more effective. You have to stay alive if you want to kill the other fellow.

General McNaughton who, as colonel, took us to France, while Chief of the Canadian General Staff between the wars, had a study made of the comparative effectiveness of the battle-seasoned Canadian Corps and the unblooded American Army during the last Hundred Days. The Corps was seventy thousand strong and the Americans had half a million troops in the line; but the Canadian Corps broke more miles of trenches, captured more prisoners, guns and machine-guns and liberated more cities, towns and villages and more square miles of territory than the whole American Army. Those figures are given *only* for the purpose of demonstrating the superiority of the craftsman over the apprentice.

Green troops always hated gas. Our first gas alerts were the worst. There was a story of an English sergeant-major who on his first trip into the line slept all night in his gas mask. The first time we heard the gas siren one of our officers ordered us to climb trees beside the gun-pits. He never knew that we disobeyed that order because immediately after he gave it he returned to his dug-out. The only time we were really worried by gas was when mustard gas first appeared on the scene in 1917. I heard of it when I came back from my first leave and was told at the same time that, as a result of it, the morale of the whole army was lower than a snake's belly. There seemed to be no answer to it. A sweating man, and when the guns were in action we were all sweating, broke out in horrible blisters. No one at the time knew what the final result might be. Before long, however, we heard that generally there were no permanent effects and we were able to breathe more easily when we thought of mustard.

Gas did not play a very great part in our lives at the front, particularly after we had run into it a few times and had gained confidence in our gas masks. They were one part of our equipment that we seldom mislaid and the quartermaster had few calls for replacements unless they became defective. When we got to France we were issued with earlier types—flannel bags that went over our heads and were tucked into the tops of our tunics. They had a little piece of glass for eyepieces, but it was hard to get them on so that the little windows were near our eyes. The first improvement was a mouthpiece to breath through. Made as they were, they were subject to leakage and it took too long to get them out of their cases and over our heads. Not long afterwards we got the ones that we used for the rest of the war. They were carried on your chest, at the alert. On the alarm you could grab your nose and put the mouthpiece in your mouth in a fraction of a second. Then you were safe while you adjusted the rest of the apparatus. Though gas was introduced by the Germans it sometimes worked to their disadvantage. The prevailing winds in France are westerly. The gas that we put over stayed with them; gas that they threw at us tended to blow back where it belonged.

Sleep may seem to be an odd thing to mention in a chapter on laughter, but laughter you may remember was seen to be an emotional relief, one of the things that helped to keep us going. I have no data to support the proposition but I am sure that very few men who slept well were victims of shell-shock. The Ancient Mariner had good things to say of sleep:

Oh sleep! it is a gentle thing,
Beloved from pole to pole!
To Mary Queen the praise be given!
She sent the gentle sleep from Heaven,
That slid into my soul.

We were healthy young animals and most of us slept well when we had the opportunity, even some who thought that they did not sleep well. I think particularly of one of our boys at Passchendaele. Our sleeping quarters were rather primitive. We could not dig a dug-out because the best ground was like jelly and would just fill in again. We could not build much above ground because the structure would sink into the muck. We made two-man shelters behind our guns by laying two duckboards side by side in the mud. Then we filled sandbags with mud and piled them around the duckboards. A sheet of corrugated iron over the top completed a home-from-home for two gunners. We would crawl in soaking wet, as we always were at Passchendaele, and go off to sleep. If you turned over in the night your shoulder scraped the iron roof. If you lit a cigarette and dropped the match through the slats of the duckboard it sizzled out in the slime underneath. Some mornings that fall we woke to find our blankets stiff with frost and looked out to see a thin layer of ice on the mud outside.

One morning the gunner with whom I shared one of those shelters crawled out of his blankets in a very bad humour, which not even the smell of frying bacon at the cook-house close by seemed to lessen. Not one wink had he slept the night before, he insisted, and how could a man be expected to fight a war if he couldn't get any sleep? That was a legitimate beef but was based on a false premise. Bob had

87

slept and I told him so. He contradicted me vigorously: not a wink, he maintained. Then I told him something that nearly broke his heart. About ten-thirty the night before the sergeant-major had come round with the rum jar. I had my issue and then tried to waken Bob. I could not do it. Even the magic words, "Rum, Bob, rum," would not rouse him. Finally I shook him so hard that I bumped his head against the sandbags. Bob never got that rum ration. And I did not get his issue either although I suggested to the sergeant-major that he should leave it with me in case Bob woke up later.

I have already told you about sleeping under a firing gun. Sleeping in the saddle may not be so hard to believe. The first time I did that was near Amiens early in the last August of the war after we came down from Arras for the big push. What I tell you now is necessary to explain my need for sleep. The position we left at Arras was near the railway station with the tracks on one side and a marble yard on the other. It was felt that because we were near the station and the railway, both of which were likely to draw long-range fire from heavy guns, we should take special pains to build substantial gun-pits. The materials were handy, there was little routine firing and we went to work.

What we built were probably the finest gun emplacements of the whole war. After we dug the gun-pits we surrounded them with blocks of marble and granite. When the stone walls were high enough we put on a layer of railway rails edge to edge to support the roof. On top of that we put a layer of granite slabs, then another row of railway rails and another layer of granite. We thought that was enough but the major said, "No, put on another layer of each." I well remember the wave of protest that engulfed me when we received that order. We had been working like galley slaves fifteen hours a day, anxious to get the job done so that we could have a little repose. As the gun-pits went higher the labour increased. Railway rails are heavy things. The granite slabs were heavy, too, and had to be moved on rollers, which were not-too-round pit props. Then they had to be inched up ramps made of railway rails. We had some idea of the sweat that went into the building of the pyramids. That final layer on the gun-pits nearly broke our hearts but at last we finished it, working until eleven-thirty at night just so we would not have that gun-pit to think of when we woke up next morning.

We brewed some tea and settled back on our blanket rolls, relaxed and happy in the realization of a hard job well done and the assurance of a few days of comparative ease. At midnight, just as we were getting ready to roll in, an orderly came from the major with an order. In two hours, we were told, we would move. We were rather unhappy; those splendid gun-pits finished with so much labour and someone else was going to take them over. If we had known then what the order meant we would not have been unhappy. That order was the call that took us to the opening of the Hundred Days that finished the war. If someone had told us that night that we were really starting for home we would have told him that he was crazy. In July, 1918, it looked to us as if we would never get home.

In due time we were ready. The horses came up and the guns were pulled out of those lovely pits. When we reached the horse lines we found everyone awake following an early reveille and working like mad to get packed. Breakfast over, we finished packing and marched some eight or ten miles to a railway station. That was quite a break. When we went to the Somme it was a four-day trek. It took us two or three days to get back from there to Vimy. This time we rode on a train.

First we had to load the guns, horses and other equipment. Once on the train you would have thought that we would seize the chance to catch up on our sleep. We read, wrote letters or played poker. It was nearly midnight when we reached Amiens and it was well after midnight before we were unloaded and ready to march.

We had about eight miles to go after that. I was mounted on Minnie. The road was smooth and straight and her easy rocking-chair gait soon had me asleep. For long intervals I would sleep, then my body would start to sway and just as I was about to fall off I would wake up with a jerk and straighten up in the saddle. Then I would go to sleep again. I slept more than half of the way from Amiens to the little town where we stopped first for a couple of days before going into the line.

Some nights later I saw a whole battery asleep on the road. I have told you that when we moved we had to be fired in at our own position. At Amiens we did not range. That was part of the surprise build-up. The gun positions were checked carefully on our maps and the muzzle velocity of the old guns was measured by a system we called calibrating. To be calibrated the guns had to be taken to Vaux-en-Amienois a little north of Amiens. I got the job of taking the six guns to the testing range. We went by night and reached Vaux just as it was breaking day. I saw many more sunrises in the army than I have seen since. Just before we got there we met a battery of Second Division on the march. They had not come south by train as we had, but were completing their third night on the road. They had not spent their days in sleep. Almost the only man in the column awake was the officer in front with the map. Drivers and outriders were all asleep in their saddles and the gunners were all asleep on the limbers and ammunition wagons. Some of them were sitting up but most of them were lying on their stomachs with their heads forward and their legs dangling behind. I know how they felt when they started that last night's march to Amiens.

This story is only hearsay, but I know the man who told it to me well and I can vouch for his veracity. He was a signaller in our brigade but not in our battery. He had been at the battery observation post at Passchendaele, constantly on duty without a relief for, I think he said, seventy-two hours. When at last he was relieved he was told to go straight to the horse lines. On his way down the plank-road he passed a forward dressing station. There he saw something that he could not resist. It was a pile of stretchers. He took one from the pile, lay down on it and went to sleep. On busy fronts like Passchendaele there was a rule that only seriously wounded men urgently needing treatment were sent to the hospitals in France. The slightly wounded were evacuated as far and as fast as was possible, with perhaps only a field dressing. That left facilities and staff available for men who needed them most. Someone gave my friend a quick examination. There were no wounds or signs of haemorrhage. He was in a coma, of course, but his pulse was good and it did not seem that he was in urgent need of treatment. A ticket was tied on him marked *Blighty,* and that is where he woke up the next morning with the problem on his hands of explaining how he got there and why he should not be charged with desertion.

> Oh sleep! it is a gentle thing,
> Beloved from pole to . . .

I am sure that my friend would agree that the Ancient Mariner had something.

7: Eats

There's no sauce in the world like hunger.
MIGUEL DE CERVANTES

I wonder that I have come this far without discussing the most important subject on a soldier's mind. I have already said that we were healthy young animals but that is so true that it will stand repeating. We were actively engaged out-of-doors and food was naturally very important to us, more important by far than quarters or leaves or even the rum issue.

Before I enlisted I had heard the usual grousing complaints about the terrible food in the army. I came prepared for the worst and was agreeably surprised. When I finished my first meal in the dining-hall at Exhibition Camp in Toronto I expressed my surprise and satisfaction and was the recipient of a protest from someone seated at the table behind me who held a contrary opinion. His protest took the form of a boiled potato behind my left ear. He certainly could not have been hungry or he would not have thrown that potato.

The fact was that very little food was wasted. Even that horrible Maconochie ration somehow or other got eaten up. It was a tinned stew and nobody ate it if there was anything else to eat. The name Maconochie is still a dirty word among old sweats. And that plum-and-apple jam! It was a byword in the army. Pemberton-Billing, the maverick MP, who, I believe, eventually went to jail, had one good point for us. He talked about our plum-and-apple jam in the House of Commons. He took a can of the stuff into the House, planted

92

it on the Treasury table, opened it with an army knife and had it passed up to the Speaker. "Mr. Speaker," he said, "doesn't that smell exactly like mineral jelly?" He had something there. It did have a smell of kerosene.

One of the greatest shocks we experienced in the army was when we found out what we had for supper in England. In Canada we had had three good solid meals a day. In France our cooks managed things so that we got three solid meals a day. To do that they might have to resort to the superabundant bully beef and the biscuit can. In England we got a good solid breakfast, a good solid dinner at noon and for supper what I am about to describe. Of course there was tea. Then there was a slice of bread each, a good thick slice cut eight to the loaf, a finger of cheese and a dab of jam. That, believe it or not, is what men who had been drilling all afternoon in the open got to carry them through to breakfast. One night the brigade chaplain acted as orderly officer. When he had finished his inspection of the cook-house he asked the routine question, "Any complaints?"

"Yes, sir," said one of our signallers raising his whole six feet four from the table. "There is not enough jam."

That riled the chaplain.

"Aren't you ashamed of yourself?" he said, "A great big man like you talking about jam."

"But, sir," said the signaller, standing his ground, "If all you got for supper was a slice of bread and a dab of jam you might be interested in the size of the dab."

That chaplain did not go to France with us. We have, however, one very clear recollection of him. In our first Sunday in England he delivered a very sincere homily in which he exhorted us all to be good boys, very good boys indeed, because, as he said, "In six months every man within sound of my voice will be either killed or wounded." He paused for effect and we gaped at him in astonishment. Then someone at the back, in a stage whisper that could have been heard one hundred yards away, said, "Holy . . . *jumping* . . . Jesus!"

93

After the Vimy barrage we were pulled out and moved forward to Neuville St. Vaast to wait our turn in getting our guns over what had been No Man's Land. That was one of the difficulties with those set-piece pushes. We churned the terrain into such a mess that after the infantry had advanced and the usual rains had fallen we could not get the guns forward. At Vimy we had to wait several days while the engineers and pioneers repaired roads and built new ones over the swamp that we had created.

In due course we got orders to advance. The pioneers had built a fascine road across No Man's Land. Fascines were bundles of branches long enough when laid side by side in the mud to make a one-way road. Just at dusk we started forward, our party consisting only of our six guns and a transport wagon with rations. We had not gone very far when we found that someone had blundered. The road came to an end in front of what had been the old German line, right where our shelling had been the heaviest and where the quagmire was the worst. The first gun off the fascines demonstrated the impossibility of further progress. The horses went down into the mud to their bellies and the gun sank down to its axle. There was nothing to do but turn around and go back.

That proved to be an all-night job. The first gun showed us what we were up against. The gun was unlimbered for turning. While we were going forward the fascines worked well. As the gun turned its wheels went down between the fascines and mired. We got the six guns turned and back into Neuville St. Vaast just as day was breaking. We parked the guns and transport wagon at the crossroads, the drivers went back to the horse lines and the gunners returned to the deep dug-out we were using. I was hardly there when the sergeant-major nailed me for guard on the parked vehicles.

I asked about breakfast. It was not nearly ready, and anyway I would be relieved in two hours. I managed to wangle a slice of bread and a mug of tea from the cook. I could smell bacon frying as I left. Food was very much on my mind as I

94

guarded the guns and transport wagon. I investigated the wagon but it did not look promising. The only things on the top were in gunny sacks, bread, potatoes and canned goods. I thrust my arm into one of the sacks of canned goods and brought out a tin that had lost its label. It was about seven inches long and had a diameter of between three and four inches. I thought that it was a large-sized tin of pork and beans, which goes to prove what a bad guesser I am. I popped it into my greatcoat pocket as a reserve against emergency. I am sure that I would have searched that transport wagon much more carefully if I had known just how far away the breakfast, which I had been promised in two hours, really was.

Just before my two hours were done along came new gun teams. They were horses and drivers from the ammunition wagons and were fresh. There were no horses for the transport wagon. There was one officer in charge and there were no gunners. Someone had figured out another way to go with the guns; the rest of the gunners were to come along later. That word *later* was an understatement.

That was a long day. We took a round-about route that after many delays put us on the main road over the ridge into Vimy village. The pioneers had put it in shape for traffic but the traffic trying to use it was far beyond its capacity. Getting to the road had been a slow business, but on the road itself the jam was unbelievable. A few years ago I made the trip from Neuville St. Vaast to the top of the ridge in a motorcar in less than ten minutes. That April day in 1917 it took us from early morning until sundown to cover the same distance. When we reached the top of the ridge I saw one reason why traffic had been so slow. The long winding road down the east face of the ridge was in full view of the enemy and within easy range of their guns. Traffic had to be sent down in little groups so as not to present a solid continuous target that would mean that any shell on the road was a dead hit. I well remember the sight as I looked down from the top of the ridge waiting for our turn to go. The whole thing was a clutter of smashed guns and wagons, dead horses and dead men.

We stood at the top of the ridge a long time that evening waiting for our turn. We got down without mishap. It was our luck that none of the shells came near us. At the foot of the hill we found a guide waiting for us. He took us into the village to our designated position on a street near the front of the town. There the guns were unlimbered and the limbers placed beside them. The drivers and the horses left, also the officer who had conducted the party. His job was to get the guns in and take the drivers back. There I was with a battery all to myself, six guns, six limbers full of shells and nothing to do with them.

And there was no transport wagon. It was then ten-thirty. I had not slept for forty hours and I had had nothing to eat except a slice of bread and a mug of tea for more than twenty-eight hours. I was not thirsty, just hungry and tired.

Then I remembered my can of beans. The fact that they were cold did not enter my mind. I fished the can out of my greatcoat pocket and was glad that it was the large-sized economy can. I placed it on the gun seat and opened it with the can-opener on the back of my army knife. When it was open I was the most surprised as well as the most tired gunner in France. My tin of beans was a tin of jam; and not plum and apple, but raspberry.

My surprise did not delay me. I did not have a mess tin and spoon as my kit had gone back into the deep dug-out when we got back from the abortive advance and of course had not gone with me on guard. But an army knife is a handy tool. I was soon gobbling jam from its blade. As I neared the bottom of the tin the pace slackened but my progress remained steady. Soon I scraped the last morsel from the bottom of the tin and leaned back on the gun seat with a sigh. That probably was the most satisfying meal I ever ate.

The next think to do was to find some place to sleep. That was not much of a problem. Directly behind my gun was a house almost intact except for the hole in one wall that had been hit by a shell. Inside the house I found that the furniture had all been removed so as my blankets were five miles away I rolled up in my greatcoat on the floor. I was asleep almost before my head hit my tin hat pillow.

Sometime during the night a large shell landed in the garden outside. I did not hear the shell but was awakened by a large piece of mud, part of the flying debris, which landed on my face. I wiped enough of it off with one sweep of my hand to permit me to breathe and went back to sleep. When I woke in the morning I could not see. The mud on my face had dried overnight and was caked in my eyes, one ear and all over my face. I had not shaved in two days and my whiskers were dried into the mud. I cleared my eyes first and then my ear. Clearing my face was like pulling adhesive plaster off a hairy back.

Outside I found that my gun had been hit and had a badly split trail. Soon the gunners appeared and with them the cook. They had come in overland and had brought very little with them, so little in fact that all I had for breakfast was hardtack and tea. The biscuits, happily, were number 8s, which had a little brown flour in them and actually had a taste. There was a great variety of biscuits all identified by number. Number 4 was the hardest one and it was almost tasteless. Eating it was like gnawing a very old bone. One of our boys put it to good use. He ground it up with a hammer, soaked it in warm water and sweetened it with condensed milk bought from the canteen, which made a rather palatable porridge. Usually we had biscuits for one meal a day.

I only saw one type of German hardtack. We captured some at Amiens together with some hay cigarettes and a half barrel of *sauerkraut*. The biscuit we captured was much softer than ours and a good deal darker, as if it had some sawdust in it. I still have some of it. It was durable and has not moulded after more than forty years. For that matter our hardtack was durable, too, and never moulded either. If it did anything it rusted. It also required sound teeth.

When I enlisted I had a back tooth that needed attention. It was more than three years later, after the armistice, that I first saw a dentist in the army. Twice my teeth had been inspected. When I enlisted the doctor looked at my teeth, and before we proceeded to France our MO looked us over, including a glance into our mouths. All that the army was interested in was whether we had enough solid teeth left to chew hardtack. By the time the war was over that back tooth of mine was in bad shape.

After we had been at Habarque for some time with the artillery school and after the armistice had come along, a dentist turned up. The next morning on the nine o'clock parade men wanting to see the dentist were ordered to fall out. There were about twenty of us, and as senior NCO I was put in charge of the parade. We found the dentist installed in a Nissen hut fitted out like a lecture hall. There were rows of kitchen chairs in the body of the hut and a dentist's chair and some other equipment at the front. When the dentist found that I was a prospective victim, and not just in charge of the parade, he said that he would attend to me first. The rest of the men were seated in the rows of kitchen chairs.

When seated in the chair I indicated my back tooth. It was examined and the opinion given that it was beyond repair and should be pulled. While he got his instruments ready the dentist apologized for the fact that he could not give me any anaesthetic. His supplies had not all arrived, he said, but it looked like a simple job.

Perhaps it was a simple job. He certainly got it all out in three pieces and with three separate operations. In describing that affair, for more than forty years I have always said that when he finally got the last part of it he was seated in my lap with his foot braced on my jaw. I have almost come to believe that. It is not, however, true, though the business was grue-some enough without exaggeration. When the last root was pulled and the blood washed off my face, the dentist turned round and said, "Next." There was no next. Every last man of that outfit had gone back to the lines.

We seldom had any vegetables but potatoes, and how we longed for fresh vegetables. One day on a march behind the old German lines we passed a field of cabbages. In no time at all every man in the battery had a cabbage, holding it by the root and gnawing away at the top of it as if it were a delicacy, as in fact it was. The lack of vegetables had its effect. In the last few months of the war there was an epidemic of boils among the old-timers. Not all of us had them but a great many, including myself, had enough for the whole army. Between August and November, 1918, I had exactly forty-one boils. Two of them, about an inch and a half in diameter, were so situated that their noses rubbed when I walked. I have told you about dancing in my saddle during the last Hundred Days. I did not always dance. I made one move in that great advance riding on my tummy on a bale of hay on the transport wagon.

Another army meal that stands out in my memory was one we had at a gun position on the shores of Dickebusch Lake not far from the spot where we had our baptism of fire. Our gun-pits were built in the line of a hedge and there were hedges all about us dividing the pocket handkerchief fields. The hedges there were all berry bushes. I am unable to name them. Some called them blackberries, to me they looked like mulberries. Whatever they were they made wonderful pies. The Belgians would not eat them, which seemed strange to us for those thrifty people were not given to wasting anything that could be put to any use. The story we heard was that there was some superstition connected with those berries. If there was it was even stupider than most superstitions.

Our cook made a deal with us. There was a standing arrangement that if we did without bread for a certain time we could draw an equivalent in flour. We immediately swarmed into the hedges picking berries. There were six of us including the sergeant and we delivered a prodigious quantity of berries to the cook-house.

Then the cook proceeded to make the pie. First he took a dixie lid. A dixie was a cooking utensil about the depth and width of an ordinary pail but of oval shape so that it had about twice the capacity of a pail. Among its uses was the making of porridge and the *boiling* of tea. The lid was from two and a half to three inches in depth. Our pie was a deep-dish pie and when it was done the wonderful pastry rose up a couple of inches above the top of the dixie lid. Simple arithmetic shows that that pie was four and a half to five inches thick. We divided it into six pieces, one for each of us and nothing extra for the sergeant. That was all we had for supper that night, deep-dish berry pie and tea. I close my eyes and I can taste it still. That is one thing about the kind of life we lived at the front, the highlights stand out so vividly.

Another time that I saw a dixie under special circumstances was in front of Vimy village. In the early fall before we moved up to Passchendaele we worked for a long time preparing for an offensive that never came off, to take Lens and push on to Douai. In preparing for the push new gun-pits were built in the plain beyond the railway embankment on the far side of the village. Working parties were sent forward and our battery supplied one of them.

Our party was quartered for sleeping in old gun-pits just short of the railway embankment. The men worked at night and slept in the daytime. There had to be some kind of timekeeper, or truant officer, to see that the men did not slip away in the darkness and return to their bunks in the gun-pits, which were uninhabited during working hours except for the cook. That was my job. I am not sure that that designation was a compliment. It may very well be that my selection was based on the principle that you set a thief to catch a thief. It was well recognized that if there was any way to dodge a nasty fatigue I had thought of it and so knew what to look for. My job included periodic inspections of the bunks to see that they had no unauthorized occupants. Somehow I arranged it so that my last bunk inspection was just before the night's work was over and while the cook was preparing breakfast. That way I got a mug of half-boiled tea before I made my last trip to the working party and called time when the night's work was done.

One morning when I turned up for my tea I found a new cook in the cook-house. The cook who had been looking after us had got his leave warrant and had left us without so much as saying good-bye. One of the other cooks was sick. On the next nine o'clock parade the sergeant-major had called out, "Fall out anyone who can cook." A remount fell out. He had not even served as helper in the cook-house and no one knew anything of his capabilities. He was taken at his word and sent up to the working party to relieve the helper from the cook-house who had been filling in for the cook on leave.

I was just finishing my mug of tea and preparing to leave on my last trip to the working party when he started to make the porridge. What I saw kept me from my duties for some time. First the cook took a dixie and filled it about two-thirds full of dry oatmeal to which he added cold water until the dixie was full. Then the dixie went on the fire. Nothing short of a break-through with German infantry swarming over the railway embankment would have got me out of that gun-pit then. I watched bug-eyed as the operation proceeded. He scooped out half of the mess and put it in another dixie. Then he added cold water to both and put them back on the fire. That operation was repeated several times. It was like the miracle of the loaves and fishes; there seemed to be no limit to the amount of porridge that came out of those dixies. Before it was done the cook had every receptacle in his establishment, including dixie lids and his dishpan, full of oatmeal porridge.

We were always grousing about our cooks but they were really good fellows and did their best with what they had to work with. At the Somme something went wrong with our ration supply and for several days we had nothing to eat but bully beef and biscuits. That put a strain on the cook. For breakfast he gave us bully beef hash. That could be good on a frosty morning. For dinner we had bully beef stew. That I could never learn to like. When bully beef is stewed you get a stringy, tasteless mess that requires a real appetite to make it palatable. We had the appetite. For supper we had cold sliced bully beef. It was a bit monotonous but no one went hungry.

After several days of this we got a parcel mail, the first since we came to the Somme. Someone decided that even though rations could not be delivered properly we should have our parcel mail. Mail, it was thought, was better for morale than rations. That is debatable. For letter mail it might be true. There was only one parcel for our subsection and that was for our sergeant. The name on it was immaterial. Food in a parcel at the guns was communal property. We gathered round the sergeant knowing that if the parcel contained food we had a proprietary interest in it. It was a large wooden box not quite the shape for liquor and almost certain to contain food. That is exactly what it did contain. When the box was opened we could hardly believe our eyes as we looked at the contents; it had come all the way from Vancouver, B.C., a five-pound tin of bully beef. That is all there was in the box—for soldiers who had eaten nothing but bully for over a week.

For the benefit of young people, bully beef was corned beef, the stuff one buys in wedge-shaped cans. The kind you see is not bad. Most of what we got was specially made to fill army contracts by suppliers who felt that they were performing a patriotic duty, being convinced that soldiers fight best when they are mad. You might find almost anything in a tin, a strip of skin with hair on it or a bone. One of our boys claimed that he had found a dog tag in a tin. We never quite believed that. If he had said a cowbell we might have been less sceptical. I would not eat the stuff in the dark. Sometimes on a night march we had a halt, when the horses would get their nosebags or haynets and we would get a half-tin of bully and a biscuit or two. I would put my bully beef in my mess tin, break it up with my clasp knife and then light a match and examine it before I ate it.

After a while we got a break at the Somme. The cook got some rice and a box of raisins. That was a big day for us in more ways than one. Our flash-cover there was inadequate and from previous shelling we knew that our position was well known. Early that afternoon the counter-battery people opposite decided that it was a good day to exterminate us. As soon as the shoot started we got the order to scatter and in no time at all we were away to the flank. As I left our gun-pit I heard one coming and went down flat. That is the only time in the war that I saw an enemy shell before it burst. Just as it hit the ground it slowed down and I saw the big ugly brute for a fraction of a second not more than seven feet from my head. When the debris had cleared away I found that my head was within two feet of the edge of the shell hole. It was a nice shell hole, too, four or five feet deep and about eight to ten feet in diameter. When we got back after the shoot we found our battery position pockmarked with shell holes like that but not a gun or an ammunition pile hit. That was very satisfactory but made us wonder how often our own shells did nothing but scare people.

While we gunners had abandoned our guns on orders, the cook, bless his greasy old soul, had stuck to his dixies. The cook-house was in the dead centre of the battery line in an old trench not more than thirty yards from the guns. It was directly in the line of fire and just where it might easily be hit by an over, something that often happened if the gun-layer was careless with his bubble. But the cook would not move. He had that rice and those raisins and we were going to have them for supper instead of bully beef, and no so-and-so Germans were going to stop him. When we got back from the flank we found supper almost ready and soon we had it. There were great piles of fluffy white rice studded with raisins so close that they almost touched each other. Mess tins were piled high and there were unlimited seconds. That rice was one of the gastronomical highlights of the war.

Parcels were always an event. Sometimes they came in droves. Christmas, 1916, was a stand-out. We were in the deep dug-outs of Vimy that I have mentioned. We were having it easy after the Somme and as the front was quiet there was no transport problem. The parcels came in wagonloads. They were piled around our dug-out so that we could hardly move. We saved them all for Christmas. Then what a time we had opening them, helped along, as you will hear in due course, by a little champagne. Practically every parcel contained a tin of canned turkey and a can of plum pudding and there were nuts and raisins and figs and dates and piles of chocolate bars. For days after Christmas we gave the cook a rest and, except for breakfast, ate nothing but canned turkey and plum pudding, which we heated ourselves in our fireplace.

For some reason unknown to me the army was hungry for toast. It was not because of the quality of the bread. Even when we were in Canada eating regular baker's bread the craving was evident. There was a large round stove in our mess hall at Exhibition Camp in Toronto. At every meal it would be surrounded by a group toasting bread. The size of the group was limited by the number who could find a spot on the outside of the stove to hold a piece of bread against. The same thing was done with the stovepipe, which was covered with bread as high up as anyone could reach. Most of that bread had more soot than crispness when it was taken away to be buttered.

You would see similar sights in France. If we had a fire in the gun-pit and had bread, there would be a circle around the brazier, each man toasting his slice of bread on the point of his knife. Army bread deserves a word. All things considered it was not bad. It had, however, its peculiarities. It came to us in gunny sacks, sometimes as much as thirty days after it was baked. It was fairly fresh even after that interval because of its special ingredients. What they were I cannot tell you but rumour said that there was a large percentage of potato. Some people insisted, wrongly I am sure, that the keeping qualities of the bread were attributable to a percentage of sawdust in the dough. The loaves were round objects like cannon balls though not quite as hard. There was a good, thick, brown crust that after some time in the gunny sack was apt to adhere to the bag. Often it had to be ripped loose and when that was done the loaf had a perceptible whisker-like addition of manilla fibre.

Sometimes our bread froze. It did that often in the winter of 1916/17, the coldest in France since records have been kept. In a regular position the cook handled the problem easily by thawing, but for a working party away from the lines for a few days and drawing separate rations it was a nuisance. One party I heard of cut up a loaf for ten men with a hand saw.

With all its faults it was still white bread and was highly regarded in a world where nearly all bread was black. The first night that we slept among civilians after making the break-through a farmer's wife saw a crust of our bread in the hands of one of my gunners. It was a disreputable-looking crust that had been in his haversack for a couple of days and had lost whatever appeal it might ever have possessed. She grabbed it from his hand and holding it high ran through the farm building shouting, *Du pain blanc! Du pain blanc!* She had not seen any white bread in more than four years and for her it was a symbol of liberation. She ran around the buildings showing it to everyone and then brought it back to its owner. Her gratitude, when he made her a present of it, would have been ludicrous if it had not spoken so eloquently of the four years she had spent behind the enemy lines.

Earlier that night we had seen our first liberated civilians. We were not the first allied troops they had seen for infantry had been through some time before, but they were still warm

105

with events of the day. It was pouring with rain as we passed through the village but they swarmed out into the street, dancing and singing and handing up cups of acorn-chicory coffee. It was unsweetened and black but if the spirit that went with it had turned up in the flavour it would have been unrivalled by any nectar in the world. I cannot ever recall being as excited and happy as those poor peasants were that night. I was not even annoyed by the old woman who nearly pulled me off my horse getting me down to kiss me. The young ones unfortunately had all been taken away by the retreating Germans, who left no one behind who could work in a factory.

A delicacy regarded more highly even than toast was fried bread. At the horse lines we could get it with our breakfast. We lined up and went by the kitchen with our mess tins. At the first stop we got porridge, thick he-man oatmeal, without sugar or milk. Next we got our bacon, on top of the oatmeal. Then we got a slice of bread and our tea. The bread was usually dry in the morning though sometimes there was jam. At supper we had margarine, occasionally even butter. If it happened that there was jam and you wanted fried bread you scraped the dab of jam from the slice of bread onto the porridge. Then you had a clean piece of bread for frying. The sergeant-cook supervised that. He stood beside a large pan of bacon fat, a pan about three feet square and four to five inches deep. I doubt if it was ever emptied. In it was an accumulation of the fat from many mornings of bacon frying, less only the amount withdrawn in the frying of bread. The fat was piping hot and at least three inches deep. You dropped your slice of bread into the bacon fat and it disappeared. The cook stood beside the pan with a large sieve-like spoon in his hand fishing out slices of bread. Whenever he got a slice that was done he gave it to the first man in line and then started fishing for another.

A slice that was done was a rich brown, crisp through and through and fit for a king. No king with a soldier's appetite could ask for anything better. One morning I had something extra. There were civilians near us and one old lady had a hen that so far no soldier had succeeded in stealing. Occasionally she had an egg for sale. Once I was the lucky purchaser. I paid her a franc and a half for that egg, thirty cents, a day-and-a-half's pay. The next morning I carried it tenderly to the cook. He broke the shell on the edge of the pan and dropped the egg into that three inches of bacon fat. My heart was in my mouth. Would he ever find it again? I got my fried bread and waited while he fished around for the egg. Finally he found it and I left with a well-fried egg nestling on top of my slice of fried bread.

Our water was good if you overlooked the tang of saltpetre that rumour said was added before we got it. Saltpetre was supposed to suspend our interest in the opposite sex. If, in fact, it was added, it was a waste of money. We drew our water from the Red Cross in water carts. I never heard of any illness in France that could be traced to bad water. Just before we went back to Vimy in the spring of 1917 we had our guns for a few days in the village of Ablain-St. Nazaire. There one of our boys got a parcel. It was incredible what came out of some of those parcels. That parcel had a bottle of water purifier in it.

We had no need of the stuff but the claims on the bottle intrigued us. All you had to do was put some of that powder into water, and no matter how bad and contaminated it might be it would almost immediately be pure and healthful or, to use Edward Gibbon's favourite adjective for good water, salubrious. My gun crew stopped getting water from water carts and started drawing it from a well in the village. After a few days something quite unexpected came up in the bucket. Some of you may know that the French army started World War I with a very striking but impractical uniform consisting of a bright blue greatcoat and a pair of red, baggy pantaloons. One day the bucket came up with a pair of those red pantaloons in it. We could not have been more startled if the last wearer of those pantaloons had still been in them. We went back to the water that came up in the water cart.

The last meal that I remember distinctly in France was a breakfast in October, 1918. The breakfast was in the barn of one of those farm lay-outs with the house on one side of the manure pile and the stables and barns on the other sides. We slept in the house, which was unoccupied except for us. My gun crew had a bedroom with a feather bed in it. Two of my gunners had beaten me to the feather bed and I slept on the floor with the other gunners. In the middle of the night a shell hit the peak of the roof and blew out quite a chunk. That called for a council of war. Some suggested a retreat to the cellar. The majority voted against a move but the two men in the feather bed decided to move anyway. This time I was one of the first into the feather bed.

In the morning the cook had a surprise for us. The travelling kitchen was in the yard but the cook slept in the stables, which had also been hit during the night. When daylight came he found a bed of mushrooms in those musty old stables, a prodigious bed of them. That morning we had bacon smothered in mushrooms, so many in fact that we could not eat them all.

Some pages back I told of descending the winding road down the easterly face of Vimy Ridge on my way to my all-jam supper. No one who saw that road during the fortnight following the capture of the ridge will ever forget it.

The next summer, when the King inspected the Canadian Corps on Dominion Day he was taken to the top of the ridge and shown the road. Somebody probably described it as I saw it that evening. Perhaps he was shown pictures. He swore a good sailor's oath and said, "There must be a memorial to the gallant Canadian Artillery." And there was. I know because I helped to build it.

A site was selected on the right-hand side of the road just short of the crest. The top of the ridge would have been under direct observation. We built a cement base rising some feet above the ground and on it was erected a large cement cross. Each day while it was being built one battery had to supply a GS wagon to haul materials, an NCO and some men. The day our battery supplied the working party I was the NCO. By that time the work was pretty well on and it was beginning to show above the sky line. The Germans could not quite make out what it was but to be on the safe side they took the odd shot at it. A few shells came over the day we worked at it. Before it was finished one gunner at least was killed by shellfire while working on his own memorial.

8: A Broken Pledge

The vow that binds too strictly snaps itself.
ALFRED, LORD TENNYSON

In my introduction I mention the pledge that was extorted from me at an early age. The phrase was "signing the pledge," but my first pledge was given long before I could write. It was extorted from me again at frequent intervals no doubt because it was felt, with a good deal of justification, that I had made the vow before I understood it or could be considered to be bound by it. When I say extorted I do not mean that there was any duress. But looking back on it now it seems to me that one of the principal activities of our Sunday school teachers was getting little boys to sign the pledge.

My pledge was well kept for a long time. I doubt that the pledge itself is entitled to much of the credit, which must go I think to the temperance lectures and exhortations that preceded the signing. When I enlisted I had never consciously tasted alcohol. I had, it was true, tasted my grandmother's Burdock Blood Bitters, which the old lady insisted was all that kept her alive. Neither she nor I knew that her tonic was about ninety per cent alcohol. All through my training I adhered to my principles and pledge. Often I went out with the boys in the evening and had a cup of coffee every time they had a beer. I have, by actual count, consumed as many as thirteen cups of coffee in one evening and then returned to camp where I slept like a rock. (That was many, many years ago.) I went to France, had my baptism of fire at Ypres, went through the Somme, was out on rest for a couple of

110

weeks near Aubigny and went up into the line again in front of Vimy Ridge; never once did I have a drink or so much as touch a rum ration. Then on Christmas Eve I fell.

It was not much of a fall, hardly more than a slip but, as the old temperance lectures used to say, it is the first drink that opens up the broad roadway that leads to destruction. Someone in the gun crew had got hold of a bottle of champagne and we drank it Christmas Eve. I took my share. I remember it vividly, that bubbling champagne in my army mess tin. My hand was steady to the eye but I could feel a quiver in my arm as I stood with the others before drinking, with the Devil himself in that mess tin. What a pleasant drink it turned out to be. If you want to have a really good drink, try a good brand of champagne in an army mess tin below ground in a gun-pit in front of Vimy Ridge. To have it at its best it must be on Christmas Eve.

There being no chronological sequence to these pages I will go from my first drink to my last memorable one in France. I say memorable because there were plenty of others after it but they were commonplace: rum issues, the odd *vin rouge* in an *estaminet* and the watery *schiedam* in Brussels. That last merits more attention and will appear again later. The memorable event was my last Christmas in France.

There must be a few words of introduction. When we were taken out of the line near Mons early in November to supply horses and equipment for the Corps School we were each given a month's pay. That sounds like a lot of money if you do not know that we drew only twenty cents a day in the field. The balance of our pay was held in our pay books against the day when we should go on leave. That meant a pay of thirty francs for gunners and drivers. For sergeants who had a position in life to support there was an extra twenty francs, making a total of ten dollars. When we were in the line with nothing to do but gamble that extra meant only that a sergeant could stay longer than a private at the crown and anchor board before he was wiped out.

111

The first night in those classy bunkhouses at Habarque I got into a poker game. It was one of those games when I held good hands but they were all second best. As you know, that is worse than no cards at all. When I got down to my last halfpenny I quit and kept the halfpenny as a souvenir.

Then a few days later came the armistice, sneaking up on us and leaving me without the means to finance a celebration. I had always promised myself that if I lived to see the armistice I would get drunk, gloriously, uproariously drunk, and make it a day to remember. I had been tipsy a few times before that but those occasions had been more or less accidental, as you may judge when you hear of them, and they were not what I planned for months and years before the end of the war. And there I was with a halfpenny in my pocket and the unpleasant prospect of having to borrow something to cover the day's rare needs and to postpone the special celebration until Christmas, when we would all get an extra fifty francs from that credit balance in our pay books.

There had been a rumour, as often before, that the Germans were about to quit but we had been fooled so many times that we were sceptical. It was not until the word came through on Sunday night that the Kaiser had abdicated that we began to take notice. Monday morning after stables and breakfast we paraded as usual at nine o'clock just, we thought, for another day of gun and harness cleaning. Roll was called and in due course the sergeant-major turned the battery over to the major. He cleared his throat a couple of times and then read the armistice order. In two hours the war would be over. It was a beautiful autumn day, sunny but with a slight haze and the air was crisp. At that moment a Frenchman away down in the valley on the other side of Habarque blew the Marseillaise on a cornet. The major stopped until the cornet's last note died away. Then he announced that there would be no more parades that day except of course stables at noon and again at five o'clock.

We were dismissed and most of us went to the bunkhouses. It was an odd feeling, quite unlike anything I had anticipated. No parades, no more war, going home soon completely intact; and no money in my pocket but a halfpenny. I sat on the side of my bunk and stared at the man across the way sitting on the side of his bunk and I tried to grasp what it meant. Then I realized that I was in financial straits. It was too early in the day to start the celebration that I had planned but it was not too early to make some financial preparations for the afternoon and evening.

I was planning my campaign for finances when along came old Buck, the farrier-sergeant. He had shod a team of horses for a farmer on the other side of the village and had been told that if he came around to the farmhouse for his money he might get something to wet his whistle. Shoeing horses for farmers was a personal perquisite to which shoeing-smiths felt that they were entitled and from which they managed to pick up a little extra cash. Buck thought that that might be a good day to collect and added that if I went along I might get something to wet my whistle, too. The idea appealed to me, two ideas to be exact. One was the free drink and the other was the companionship of a fellow sergeant with some extra money in his pocket.

Away we went. The farmer greeted us rapturously. He, of course, had heard the news. If Buck had brought the whole battery with him I think the farmer would have tried to wet all our whistles. We were invited into the kitchen and given chairs. Then the farmer pulled up a trap door in the tiled floor and went down into a pit that served as a cellar. Presently he emerged with a bottle. It was so covered with dust and cobwebs that we could not read the label but it was wired and that gave us hope. When it was opened it turned out to be champagne. The farmer brought two glasses and filled them. We insisted that he bring a third. He demurred at first but at last got a glass for himself and filled it about half-way. We all took a drink and the farmer burst into song. The champagne was good and I do not remember anything about the singing or the song except that it had frequent references to *La Raypoobleeque*. Buck and I finished the bottle and came away. Neither of us remembered that the money for shoeing the horses had not been paid. I am sure that Buck went back for it later.

My financial problem was still unsolved and I left it that way. It was then time for stables. The armistice and that half bottle of champagne were all the stimulation I needed that day. I postponed my big celebration until Christmas.

In due course Christmas arrived. We got our regular pay and our extra fifty francs Christmas money and I was all set. On Christmas Eve six of us went out together to an *estaminet*. We were moderately temperate, if you know what I mean, and confined our drinking to red wine, just enough to make our singing sound good to us and to give the lights that nice rosy tinge. When we left we bought three bottles of champagne, just for an eye-opener in the morning.

The bottles of champagne were given to me to keep. That, I feel, was rather flattering. Not everyone in the army could be trusted with the custody of communal liquor. I took the bottles with me and put them under my pillow; we actually had straw-filled canvas pillows and palliasses at Habarque.

Because it was Christmas reveille did not blow until seven o'clock the next morning. The horses must have missed us and been puzzled by our being an hour later than usual with our currycombs and feed bags. My five friends gathered at my bunk and we started the day by drinking the champagne. That is one way to start Christmas with a bang. Six of us drank three bottles of champagne, smacked our lips and went out to look after the horses. After breakfast it was announced that there was English beer in the canteen. Anyone who has tried to drink French *bière*—they cannot even spell it let alone make it—will know what good news that was. As there were no parades that day except stables, we spent the morning pegging away at the English beer just to keep the champagne from getting lonely. Dinner was at noon, a bang-up affair with plum pudding and all the trimmings such as we had not seen since we left home. After dinner we went back to the canteen again. Up to this time I had made no plans for the evening. As it turned out I did not need any.

Suppertime came around and I went to the sergeants' mess. That was part of the swank of the Corps School. The attendance was very slim. Some of the boys had saddled up in the afternoon and ridden to a neighbouring town where they could get eggs and chips and spend the evening away from the line. There were only six of us left. That number, though important to what followed, was definitely not known to the officers. Just as we finished our meal an orderly came from the officers' mess with a present for the sergeants, four bottles of "Black & White" whisky.

Quite some time later I went back to the bunkhouse. I had had more than half a bottle of whisky and it had had the desired effect. I cannot say what time it was but, though the lights were still on, the canteen was closed. We had a lot of fun in the bunkhouse but what we did seems somehow to be veiled in a pink fog. My memory, however, is very clear on one thing, the last episode for me, I am told, of the evening. I was down on my hands and knees on the floor. One of my drivers was down on his hands and knees facing me. I would stick out one leg and wag it like a tail and say, "Woof, woof." My companion would stick out one leg, wag it like a tail and say, "Woof, woof." That went on for some time. It was shortly after that that my gang thought that I ought to be in bed and put me there. I had fulfilled my ambition to celebrate the armistice properly.

Reveille sounded at six o'clock the next morning, its usual hour. I was glad that they had not bothered to undress me when they put me to bed. And oh, how I hated horses.

Each time I have written the word *champagne* I have thought of a story told to me by a friend who saw service in the railway troops. He was working on construction on the Somme front in March, 1918, when the Germans made the great break-through that very nearly split the allied armies. Being unarmed and untrained for combat the railway troops fell back in considerable disorder. At Albert they were rallied and with other disorganized groups formed into emergency battalions, equipped with small-arms and rushed back to the front to help stem the tide while reserves were being brought in. On the road they were passed by Australians being rushed up from reserve. The Aussies were mechanized, equipped with the improvised motor machine-gun outfits we saw sometimes later that year. The equipment consisted of ordinary motor lorries with thin armour rising at the sides about four feet above the floors of the lorries. There were machine-guns mounted and the gunners were supposed to be behind the plates of armour.

I said *supposed* to be behind the armour. They were not, and without unloading they could not have taken advantage of their armour. The night before they had stopped at a deserted *château*. It had been occupied until word of the break-through was received and then it had been abandoned in haste. The Aussies found the wine cellar intact and well stocked. Even Aussies have limits to their capacity and when they had to move on at daybreak there was a large part of the stock of the wine cellar unconsumed. If you know soldiers, and particularly if you know Australian soldiers, you do not have to be told that the treasure-trove was not left behind. It was piled into the lorries behind the armour to protect it from stray bullets and other mishaps and was piled higher than the top of the armour. My friend says that it was all champagne. That is only surmise. At least the cases above the armour were champagne. On top of the wine were the machine-gunners preparing their weapons for battle. My friend tells me that four lorries passed him loaded like that and that they roared on east, the gunners flexing their muscles and prepared to stop the whole German army.

Having dragged into this narrative, by the ears as it were, a second-hand story I might as well drag in another. It might well have appeared in a later chapter on leave but as it does have some alcoholic aspects perhaps this is the proper place for it. Another friend of mine, a gunner in one of the batteries in our brigade, got his leave warrant while we were on the Ypres front with horse lines at Vlamertinghe. The pass was very welcome but there was one fly in the ointment. My friend's riding breeches had seen long service and were certainly far from fit to be worn to London on leave. Uniforms and equipment have a way of wearing out and where they wore out first depended a bit on the branch of the service. The infantry used to say that with them it was $\mathcal{C}$ the boots that gave way first but that in the artillery the vulnerable point was the seat of the pants. After more than forty years that can be ignored. At any rate my friend's breeches were very bad and a man could not very well go on leave to London with an empty sandbag over his arm to spread out if he wanted to sit down on something cold.

The battery quartermaster-sergeant had no breeches in stores that would fit my friend but he was helpful. The quarter-bloke of X battery, he said, had a new shipment of Bedford cords and was sure to have something that would fit. He would arrange that if my friend went over with a five-franc note he would get a pair of breeches that would be a credit to the artillery. My friend readily agreed. That night after supper he walked over to the X battery where he found the quarter's stores were closed. He hunted up the quarter-bloke's bivy, which was in a hut sunk partly into the ground as protection from flying splinters, covered with tent canvas and with a rubber groundsheet as a curtain at the door. My friend was pulling aside the groundsheet when he was interrupted by a hoarse voice.

"Have you got the dough?" said the voice.

The five-franc note was passed through the opening and then an arm came out at the end of which was a hand holding two canteens, or water bottles, by the leather straps. These certainly were not pants. My friend, however, was a man of keen intuition and he accepted the substitution without demur. As he hurriedly left the hoarse voice followed:

"And don't come back. That's the last you'll get."

My friend had not intention of going back, especially after he had pulled one of the corks and confirmed the opinion he had already formed, that instead of mundane things like pants he had two canteens filled with rum. Some time and several swigs later he was standing smacking his lips and replacing the cork of one of the bottles when two figures emerged out of the murk, one walking behind the other.

"Hey, guys," hailed my friend. "Wanna drink?"

The leading figure stalked on without any indication that he had seen or heard anything. The man behind shook his head violently but said nothing. That did not make sense. A soldier who did not want a drink! After pondering that implausible possibility for some time my friend decided that there must have been some misunderstanding. He ran after the pair and repeated the offer. Again it was ignored and rejected. Now my friend was sure that he must be so drunk that he could not make himself understood. He tried a third time. He got well in front of the pair. As he turned to renew his offer the moon peeked through the clouds and he saw something that he had not seen before. The figure in front was that of a staff officer with his red tabs on his tunic and the insignia of the Guards, the man behind was a private and quite obviously the officer's batman. That discovery very nearly sobered my friend.

He has often wondered since why he did not land in the clink that night. If he had been in the Imperial lines he would most certainly have been in the guardhouse in no time at all. But the Imperial staff officer was in Canadian lines and felt perhaps that it was none of his business. Likely he had the general Imperial feeling that the colonials were a queer lot who in spite of their apparent lack of discipline always seemed to pull their weight when they were needed. I have seen traces of smiles around the corners of the eyes of Imperial officers more than once, which I am sure were followed by amusing anecdotes later in the mess. But I have felt, too, that those smiles were often of half-approving amusement.

Some pages back I mentioned the fact that a couple of times I was tipsy accidentally. One of those episodes took place at Wallers on the way to Mons and the last place where we fired our guns. After we covered the advance beyond Wallers we halted and stood in reserve while the Corps swept forward crowding the Germans back. For a while we were billeted in the town. Quite often after we got behind the old lines we slept in houses, sometimes even in beds. At Wallers my corporal and I were in a feather bed. The household where my subsection was billeted was made up of three old people all about eighty years of age. There was the old man and his wife and her sister. All the males of an active age had been taken away by the retreating Germans.

The house consisted of two large rooms both with tile floors. There was the kitchen-living-room where my gunners and drivers slept on the floor and there was a bedroom with two large feather beds. All the time we were there the old man slept in a chair in the kitchen. Nothing could induce him to go to bed. We were honoured guests and some of us must sleep in one of the feather beds. So my corporal and I slept in one of the feather beds in one corner of the room while the two old ladies slept in a feather bed in the other corner. I hope those old people did not have too much trouble delousing that feather bed after we left.

One day and night I was battery orderly-sergeant. Each twenty-four hours in every battery there was an orderly officer assisted by an orderly-sergeant. The duties included inspections and the mounting of the guard and piquet. The last duty at night if there was no disturbance to interrupt one's slumbers was the pleasant task of supervising the rum issue. If the weather was good when we were in cushy billets like Wallers there was no general issue but only a tot for the guard and piquet. No doubt the rum provided for each unit was sufficient for an issue each day for every man in the field;

119

but so much disappeared in unauthorized uses that, by the time it had passed through all the hands that had it in charge between the base and the ultimate consumer, it had so diminished in quantity and often in quality, by dilution, that it was not sufficient for a daily ration. It is not only in civilian life than one hears of exorbitant middleman profits.

My orderly officer that night was a large, genial extrovert. When I reported to him for the rum issue he got out the large earthen jar that rum came in and suggested that we ought to fortify ourselves for our arduous task ahead. When I had put away the generous nip he had poured for me and was about to leave to bring the guard he stopped me.

"I don't suppose," he said, "that even a sergeant can fly on one wing. We had better have another."

We did. Then I brought the members of the guard who were not on the beats at the moment and they received their issue. Before I left to relieve the men walking the beat we had another refresher. After the men on the beat were looked after we again had another refresher before I left to bring the piquet. I should explain that the men on both guard and piquet were on duty for two hours at a time and were then off for four hours. There were three men on piquet, one for each section, and they had to wait to be relieved to get their rum. After the piquet off duty at the time had been attended to we had another refresher. As we sipped it the officer had an idea.

"I don't think, sergeant," he said, "that it is necessary for you to relieve the piquet. I'll just put three issues in this jug and you can take along the fuse cap to measure it out and give the boys their ration right at the piquet lines."

By this time anything that the orderly officer said to me seemed highly sensible and I agreed. In no time at all I was on my way to the horse lines with three generous issues in a jug and with the brass cover of a shrapnel-shell fuse to use as a measure and cup. As I approached the piquet line in the dark I heard two of the piquet, from my own subsection, too, conspiring against me.

"We won't tell Ernie," one of them said to the other, "that we sneaked away and had our rum with the rest of the piquet. Then we'll get an extra issue."

That was a startling proposition. Perhaps the word had leaked out that the orderly officer and I were having a ball. But the matter had very serious aspects. One really could not give a man on duty a double issue. That would be a grave breach of discipline and a very dangerous thing to do. The fact that I was on duty myself was quite beside the point. My duty was perfectly clear and I performed it manfully. I drank those three generous issues myself and went back to the orderly-room.

"Well, that's a good night's work done," said the orderly officer. How well done he little knew. "Suppose we have a nightcap and turn in."

Fortunately the orderly-room was not far from my billet. If it had been further I might not have made it. But make it I did and there was an exceedingly tight sergeant in the old Frenchman's feather bed that night. I hate to think of what would have happened if there had been a call for the orderly-sergeant during the night.

You may wonder how one felt on the morning after such an occurrence. It was really not as bad as you might think. Reveille was a bitter pill but one had to move so fast then that there was no time for self-pity. We were young, in good condition, adequately fed and with little on our minds. (Only occasionally did we think of the future and of the chances in the lottery of battle.) If any of my readers are interested, fresh air and exercise make the best remedy for a hangover.

I have recollections of many dismal scenes in bunkhouses and dug-outs. One is of Witley camp in England when one of our boys tried to drown his homesickness in the pubs. He was not used to it and the result was the only attack of DTs that I ever witnessed. All night long he kept us awake with loud cries of, "Hold 'em, Tizzie." Tizzie was his buddy in the next bunk. The disturbance was caused by thirty-foot snakes of many colours that were coming in the doors at each end of the bunkhouse.

One of my most vivid memories is of our sergeant-major at reveille. One of the duties of the NCO in charge of the piquet was to waken the sergeant-major before he roused the trumpeter. Piquets were corporal's jobs and I seldom had the chore because I spent most of the time up front with the guns. In our battery the sergeant-major made, and usually maintained, a claim to be the official custodian of the rum jar. As custodian he took a large part of its contents into personal, physical custody. Before retiring he would take a swig or two and then make up his cot.

Making up a bed was quite an art in the field. Most of us used what we called an envelope fold. We each had two blankets. We put them down, overlapping by about one-third, on whatever we were going to sleep on, a bunk if we were lucky, or planking, concrete, gravel in a gun-pit or just plain dirt. Then we lay down in the middle and pulled the blankets up around us so that part of each blanket was underneath and part was over and one was in a snug bundle like a mummy in its case. The pillow might be a greatcoat though in cold weather that was usually pulled over the top to seal the package, or it might be a kit-bag, or even a shrapnel helmet.

The sergeant-major had an additional detail. After he was rolled up he took the tops of his blankets over his head and sealed himself in. What air he got during the night had to seep through two army blankets. The odour that arose when one opened the sealed blankets in the morning to rouse him before reveille was something to remember. There was enough alcohol in the reek that came out when the package was opened to have burned like a torch if a match had been put to it. You may wonder why no one did put a match to him.

He was an old Imperial but he knew nothing of gunnery. In his days as a regular he had been a shoeing-smith and when he got his sergeant-major's crown he was the battery farrier-sergeant. But he had character and driving power. For the officers' purposes he was ideal. They knew that when he was given an order it would be carried out. How he got those orders I am sure they never knew. When he got a written order he would fumble in his pockets, say that he had left his glasses in his quarters and ask someone to read it for him. The old fraud did not have any glasses, nor did he have any use for them; he could not read a word. In fact he could not even spell his name. After the armistice he asked me to write a letter for him to the War Office, giving particulars of his Canadian service, for long-service pension purposes. He gave me his regimental number and I had that in the letter correctly. With him sitting beside me I spelled his name incorrectly, and he did not even know it. It was not until I read the reply to him that I found out how his name should have been spelled.

His fame extended far beyond our battery. If you say the Black Prince or Black Jack to any Third Division gunner or driver I am sure that he will know whom you mean. Certainly anyone from the Eighth Army Brigade would know it. I was his special aversion, perhaps because I got a third stripe that he wanted someone else to get. While that was pending he carried on an active campaign to make sure that I was not the one to get the promotion. If I was at the horse lines—he was never at the guns—he would wait until some of the officers were around and then go to the farthest part of the lines. Then he would shout in that sergeant-major voice, which was one of his few qualifications, "Corp'l Black, why the 'ell ain't so-and-so done?" Invariably it was something I did not have to do. I used to swear that if I ever met him in civilian life I would hunt up the closest brick and settle old scores.

I did meet him in civilian life. About a year after we got home I was driving one evening when I saw him on the sidewalk. I almost wrecked that fine new car getting stopped and parked so that I could run back and shake hands with him. I have already said something about comrades-in-arms. When he died not long afterwards I was one of those who stood at attention by his grave.

I had one drink of rum that warms me still when I think of it. It was on the morning of September third in the Hundred Days and the morning after we broke the first spur of the Hindenburg Line. Someone had devised a new tactic quite unlike anything we had done before and not unlike the tactics of World War II. Our battery was part of the force to be engaged, called in the official Canadian history the Independent Force. There were two field batteries in the group, a strong force of cavalry, the Corps cyclists and a number of the improvised motor machine-gun units like those the Aussies had used as wine carriers at the Somme. We were not told about it beforehand and took part in the opening barrage. After the first few range lifts in the barrage our horses came up and the guns were moved out into the road. There the major told us what was afoot. One of the obstacles in front of us was the Canal du Nord. When the infantry reached it they were to cover the bridge across it with their machine-guns to prevent its destruction. Then the cavalry was to dash across followed by the rest of the Independent Force. There we were to fan out and shoot up and disorganize the rear lines while the infantry followed over the bridge and spread out for a further advance. That would be our second time in front of the infantry.

As soon as we heard the nature of the job there was a great scramble for weapons. Field batteries in World War I were not liberally equipped with small-arms. There were two rifles strapped on the shield of each gun. They were used only for guard duty and occasional, unscheduled target practice. There was a small amount of rifle ammunition. Our leather bandoliers were designed to carry cartridges, but I never saw any in them or anything but cigarettes or chocolate bars. Most of us had lost our bandoliers. The officers had revolvers. Otherwise the battery was unarmed except for

124

our eighteen-pounders. In a few minutes we were like an arsenal. A main road through an active battlefield is an easy place to arm. With open warfare behind the enemy lines facing us we appropriated anything lethal that we could lift. We had not gone very far on the road, inching our way to our rendezvous, before we were armed to the teeth. Almost every man had a rifle, while ammunition in canvas bandoliers hung from everyone and from various parts of the gun and limber. We had boxes of Mills bombs piled on all the limbers and ammunition wagons. This was open warfare in earnest.

After getting forward a mile or so we halted behind a slight crest by the side of the road where we dismounted and waited for the order to dash forward and make history. That order never came. We heard various rumours about what had happened up in front but no two stories were the same except that all agreed that the leading units had been cut to pieces.

That night we slept around our guns. That is not quite correct. Most of us slept in the open field but some of us, including me, sought shelter in an old trench a few feet in front of our guns. It was a battered trench and nothing looks worse than last week's trench especially if it was the scene of smart fighting when it was last occupied. Shortly after we arrived it was filled by infantry on their way up to jump through the front-line troops in the morning and carry on the attack. In due course I settled down to sleep. It was a bright moonlit night and cold. Using my tin hat as a pillow I curled up with my legs pulled well into my greatcoat and was soon fast asleep. As I slept I relaxed and my legs straightened out beyond the skirt of my coat. I became cold and woke up. The artillery greatcoat was what was called a British warm and was shorter than the infantry coat. A short coat does not make a good blanket; several times during the night I had to re-curl.

My companions had longer coats and for the most part slept better than I did and none of them seemed to be bothered by the thought that before dawn they would be on the move to pass through the front line and carry on the advance. There was no sign of day when they were aroused. While they wriggled into the web equipment that carried their packs and all of the hardware and paraphernalia that made up a foot soldier's outfit, an officer came along the line with a rum jar. The moon had gone down and it was quite dark. He did not realize that I was an interloper until after he had handed me a tot. Then for the first time he noticed the big brass guns on my sleeves.

"Oh, you don't get that," he said, reaching for the brass fuse cap that he had just handed me.

I gulped the rum and handed back the empty fuse cap. The officer laughed and went on with his pleasant chore. Presently the infantry departed. Up to the time they left they had had no breakfast. Perhaps before they jumped off there were some dixies of hot tea for them and perhaps some porridge for their mess tins. I marvel at the people at home who begrudged those men their tot of rum and who wrote indignant letters to the newspapers protesting against "our brave lads being sent into battle half-drunk." I have relished that drink in my memory scores of times since; many of those boys have had no such recollections for it was their last drink.

There was another single drink that I remember gratefully. It was just after we came out of Passchendaele. We had had six weeks of it and were out on rest at Verdrel, half-way up the ridge behind Barlin. As usual after a long time on a nasty front I had a reaction. While I was in the line I stood it I think as well as the next man. When I got out of the line there was a let-down. I would run a small temperature, have a bit of headache and perhaps a digestive upset. It only lasted a day or two. When it came on after Passchendaele I reported sick and was put in charge of the sick parade. Our MO was on leave. He was replaced by Jack Maynard, the old Varsity football great. After the men had all been examined and disposed of he turned to me.

"What's your trouble, corporal?" he said.

I told him.

"I know just what you need," he said. He reached into his hip pocket, brought out a large silver flask filled with Scotch whisky and then prescribed. "Take all of that you can drink without choking."

I had never drunk neat whisky before but my natural talents must have amazed him. I am proud of the fact that I did not parade sick again the next day just to get another dose of that perfect medicine.

On another occasion I had liquor given me medicinally but that time it was not prescribed by the MO. Early in 1918 the world suffered an epidemic of influenza. I have heard civilians describe the situation at home at that time. One of them said that it must have been almost as bad as being at the front. We had it at the front, too.

We had our guns in a village in front of Lens when the epidemic struck us. In no time at all our ranks were thinned more than they ever were in action. Our guns were manned by skeleton crews, two or three men to the gun, and things got so bad that even I was acting sergeant-major at the guns for some time. The worst cases went to hospital and the light ones were handled right in our lines. The dressing station was swamped. There for days at a time men lay out under the trees on stretchers.

One morning I had the early symptoms of flu and reported that fact to the captain. There was no telling when the overworked MO would be available. The captain told me to get into bed and that he would be around presently with some medicine. He said bed because he knew that in that position I really had one, a stretcher in a nice dry, airy cellar, airy because a big shell had taken down part of the house and had blown out part of the cellar wall. I got into my envelope fold, sealed by my greatcoat, and waited for the captain and the medicine. Presently he came. The medicine was in a granite mug, not the largest size, which you will hear mentioned later, but the medium-sized mug, filled to the brim with neat rum. I got that down me and lay back, tucking my blankets up around my chin, and went to sleep. That was about nine o'clock in the morning; at eight o'clock the next morning I awoke for the first time, just one hour short of twice around the clock. The flu was all gone.

You have seen the name Passchendaele a number of times in these pages. If you stay with me to the bitter end you will see it often again. If in my dreams I have ever had a real nightmare about the war I am sure that Passchendaele will have been the scene of it. That was one place where we got our rum regularly and liberally except on the very rare occasions when the ration party drank most of it on the way up to the guns.

For the full appreciation of what follows it is necessary that some account of Passchendaele be given here, not of the battle itself but of the ground it was fought over. The country around was flat and low and drained by a series of canals, streams and ditches, which did the job reasonably well in peacetime. All during the war there had been heavy shelling in that area, and then during most of the summer and all of the autumn of 1917 the heaviest shelling of the war fell in that low, badly drained spot. Early in the battle all drainage was destroyed and the whole place turned into a vast quagmire. Unusually heavy rains added to the mess. Hundreds of men drowned in the mud that filled the shell holes. A look at an aerial photograph of the battlefield shows that there was scarcely a spot where shell holes did not touch each other or overlap.

To supply an army in a swamp it was necessary to build roads through the swamp. They were of two kinds. For the infantry there were duckboard paths; for the guns and transport a plank-road was built. It was constructed of heavy planks and may have been twenty to twenty-five feet in width. Being easily spotted from the air it was constantly under fire and was continually in need of repairs. The guns of course had to be placed near the road and they drew fire.

One morning at the horse lines, after coming down the night before from the guns, I was roused by the sergeant-major long before reveille had blown with the news that it was my turn to take up the ration party. We saddled up and were away long before breakfast was ready. Before leaving we did get a mug of tea and a slice of bread. I always seemed to be starting something with a slice of bread for breakfast. If we had known what was in store for us we would probably have taken some bully beef and cheese and biscuits to serve as a lunch.

We proceeded first to the depot near Ypres to draw rations for the battery. There was a long delay there and it was after lunchtime before we were on our way again. Remembering the kind of soldiers we were, I am at a loss to explain why we did not lunch on the rations we carried. We were not ready yet for raw bacon or beef, but there must have been at least one gunny sack full of month-old bread. It would have been no chore at all to rip one of those loaves loose from the sacking merged with its crust. Perhaps we were just in a hurry to get the job done. Even a soldier has times when he forgets his stomach.

Our progress was slow. We were now all dismounted and each leading two horses loaded with boxes and bags. There were delays in traffic and by the time we came in sight of the battery it was nearly four o'clock. At that point the Germans started to shell the plank-road. We unloaded our freight and piled it beside the road. I sent the drivers back with the horses to the Peggy Dump about a mile back to wait for me there. I kept one man with me to look after the pile while I walked into the battery position to get a carrying party to take in the rations. When that was done I sent Adam, the man I had kept as guard, back a couple of hundred yards to an old German pillbox to wait for me there while I got a receipt from the major for the rations. The carrying party dispersed to the guns and the cook and I stood on the plank-road while he checked my list and OK'd it for the major's signature.

As we stood there one lone packhorse came galloping down the plank-road from the front, riderless and un-attended. Some ration party up front had been caught in the shelling and dispersed. Old Mac, the cook, was much more alert mentally than I was for he saw the opportunity and grasped it while I did not even guess what was going on. He got out into the middle of the plank-road and as the packhorse passed he grasped the flying bridle. Setting his feet hard and throwing his full weight back he swung the horse off the road and onto its side in the muck. In a moment he was on the horse, undoing the surcingle and allowing two long white boxes to fall into the mud. Each of the boxes contained two large earthenware jars bearing on the side the initials SRD, spirits of rum diluted. We had four gallons of rum.

We carried the jars to the mudhole that Mac called a cook-house. I went to the major to get my ration receipt signed, intending to return to the cook-house for a bite to eat and a sandwich or two to take back to the drivers. What happened when I got back to the cook-house put all thought of food for myself or anyone else out of my mind. Part of the cook's equipment was a set of graduated granite mugs. Mac had the largest one, a pint, filled with rum for me. It was then after five o'clock and I had had nothing to eat since the night before except a mug of tea and a slice of bread before daybreak. I had been on my feet, walking or standing around, almost all day. I emptied the big mug and was on my way. Even before I reached Adam at the pillbox the stuff had begun to work. I told Adam what had happened. I can still hear him wail, "Oh, Ernie, what did you send me back for?" I remember that he had been pleased with the suggestion of the pillbox when I made it to him.

Away we went to join the drivers and the horses at Peggy Dump. Soon I was floating along, my feet scarcely touching the planks of the road. Presently a salvo of 5.9s came over. A 5.9 was a German shell approximately six inches in diameter and weighing about one hundred pounds. It dug a hole four or five feet deep and ten to twelve feet across depending on what kind of soil it landed in. Its burst, including black smoke and flying dirt, looked like a bush or small tree. Like a smart soldier, when he heard the express-train roar of the approaching salvo Adam went flat on the plank-road and was out of the way of flying splinters when the shells landed. Not me. Right after the bursts, which were close, with two on each side of the road, I took off my tin hat and made a sweeping bow to the black clouds blowing away from the shell holes. Adam did not approve. Most of his remarks I have forgotten but I do remember that he said something about a "damn fool." Away we went again. Presently we approached the Peggy Dump and the drivers. Tight as I was, before we got there I had made my plans.

"Look, Adam," I shaid, no said. "You tell the driversh to beat it back to the horshe linesh on their own and you shtay behind to help me get mounted."

When the drivers were gone Adam helped me to get my left foot into the stirrup and then with great pushing and heaving managed to get me on my horse's back. Then he went around to the other side and put my right foot in its stirrup. Have you ever ridden on a fluffy pink cloud right into a glorious sunset? Then you have no idea of the ride I had that November evening down the road through St. Jean, Wieltj and Ypres to our horse lines near Vlamertinghe.

That incident had an unhappy sequel. Poor old Mac buried his four jars of rum near his cook-house. No one but he and I knew the secret and even I did not know the location of the cache. There was great speculation in the battery as to why Mac refused to take his reliefs and insisted on staying at the gun lines. On my trips to the guns I always got

131

an extra ration but never again from the big granite mug. After eighteen days without a relief Mac was killed in his cook-house. I was then free to disclose the secret. We made a determined effort to find the rum. We probed all likely places but without success. Unless some Belgian plough has turned them out the remains of those four gallons of rum still lie buried near the Heights of Abraham in front of Passchendaele Ridge.

9: VIPs

His face is the worst thing about him.
WILLIAM SHAKESPEARE

That line from Shakespeare does not apply to all the Very Important Persons I propose to speak of but it certainly is appropriate to the first one on my list. I saw him twice. The first time was when I was at the Imperial Artillery School where I learned something of riding. We were on the road outside the town going to an open field for mounted drill when we were passed by an American staff car. Our attention was drawn to the open car when the horses all shied, perhaps at the car but possibly at the big man in olive drabs seated in the rear. I was almost as startled as the horses and felt that I had seen that big man before. In a moment I realized that it was only his picture that I had seen, scores of them. It was Irvin S. Cobb. If he were living I know that he would not object to my saying that he was ugly; he used to kid himself about it in his articles. And ugly as he was there was nothing repulsive about it. It was an arresting sort of ugliness, strong and distinctive.

I saw him next in Paris. He was billed to speak at the American leave centre and of course I went. He was the Bob Hope of the doughboys in World War I. I had read all his articles when he started out as a correspondent with the French army and wound up with the Germans, when he was overrun in one of the early battles. I had laughed when I read them but I laughed louder when the big, ugly man rehashed them for the troops. Some of his stories had more

133

point for me in Paris than when I had read them in Toronto. I knew exactly what he meant when he said that when he woke up after spending his first night behind the German lines in a cowshed previously occupied by troops he was the most densely populated spot in Belgium. He exaggerated. Take the word of an expert. He could not get that bad in one night.

My first encounter with a VIP in the army was in London on my first leave after landing in England. Most of us when on leave in London stayed at the Maple Leaf leave centre on Charles Street off Berkeley Square. It is now part of the set-up of the English Speaking Union and, if you are interested, the cafeteria in the annex is the exact location of what I am now going to describe. One morning at breakfast we were told that the King and Queen would inspect the place that afternoon. Long before the appointed hour the lounge was crowded with Canadians waiting to see their monarch and his consort. While we were waiting for the royal party a big red-headed gravel-crusher from Nova Scotia amused himself at the lounge piano knocking out "Home, Sweet Home," with one finger on each hand. The tune was barely recognizable.

Presently the King and Queen arrived preceded by an equerry. We all sprang to attention. "Carry on," said the King. We all looked somewhat blank having no idea of how one is supposed to carry on in the presence of royalty. The command was repeated and the equerry indicated that any of us who had seats were to sit down. The big redhead sat down on the piano stool. The King saw him there and said, "Carry on at the piano, please." The redhead turned on the stool and faced the keyboard but otherwise did not move a muscle. "I said," snapped the King, "carry on at the piano." This time there was no *please*. There was just a hint in the tone of his voice that he had not forgotten his years in the navy. The Nova Scotian did as he was told. With one finger on each hand he pounded a few keys that gave forth sounds

134

somewhat like "Home, Sweet Home." When he finished what little he could do he started over and kept on repeating it until the royal party left. No one smiled, not even the King, and certainly not the redhead. By the time is was all over the strip of skin above the Nova Scotian's tunic collar was redder than the thatch above.

The party circulated around the room with the royal couple addressing a few words to every third or fourth man. The Queen seemed to have a morbid interest in seasickness. Most of us were new arrivals on our landing leave and when she discovered that she had a standard topic of conversation. Presently the Queen came near the place where I was standing. There were not seats for all of us and I had had to do my carrying on standing up. The man next to me was in a big armchair. The Queen addressed herself to him.

"What part of Canada are you from?" she asked.

The soldier crossed his legs, braced his elbow on his knee, rested his chin on his palm and proceeded to tell Her Majesty of the wonders of Manitoba. The Queen's equerry nearly fainted. When he recovered he tapped the Manitoban smartly on the shoulder and explained to him the facts of life, at least in so far as they touched on the way in which one carries on a conversation with the King's consort. The conversation was completed with a very red-faced boy from the prairies standing stiffly at attention and wishing that he had never enlisted.

The last time that I saw the King the Queen was not with him. Instead, he had Field Marshal French for company. For young readers, Lord French commanded the British Army in France for the first few months of the war but was then in command of home forces and the armies in training. The occasion was the final inspection of the Third Divisional Artillery to which we belonged before we proceeded to France.

We were rather annoyed with the King that day. After all the work we had done, shining up for the occasion, he hardly looked at us. During the march-past he did not look at us at all. He barely acknowledged the salutes. He sat his horse, which was about a third of a length ahead of Lord French's mount, talking over his shoulder to the Field Marshal. Later in the day we learned the reason for his indifference and forgave him. That was July first, 1916. If you remember your history you will know that was the day that the British and French armies kicked off at dawn to open the Battle of the Somme. It was then about eleven o'clock in the forenoon and the King and Lord French were no doubt discussing the earliest fragmentary reports from the front. Even at that early hour the news could not have been good.

My next VIP, and for me the most important, was our colonel. Not many colonels are VIPs; some even are not human. This colonel, however, was different. He is known today as General Andrew G. L. McNaughton, the man who trained and for a while commanded the Canadian Army in World War II.

We saw him first at Bramshot, our first English camp, in the open field at the northwest corner of the camp, where the four miles of maple trees planted as a memorial to the Canadians by the parish of Bramshot came to an end. We were all in the field, the whole four batteries of the brigade, before the new colonel appeared. He understood the business of a dramatic entrance. As we waited he galloped onto the field with the long cloak he wore floating behind him in the wind. That dramatic entrance by our new colonel, returned from France to make soldiers of us and then to take us back with him to the war, may have been an accident, but I do not think it was. It was entirely in line with what we learned of him later, his knowledge of what a soldier likes, what he can do and how he can be induced to do that to the utmost. And in due course we found that he could rough it like the rest of us when the going was tough.

His first orders came out the same day. We really knew then that we had a new colonel. Reveille was advanced an hour. That made quite a stir for a few days. Then we rather grew to like it. We were the hardest-worked brigade in the division. We did not grouse about that; we boasted of it. It is the sign of a real leader that he could set a hard, exacting task and get cheerful obedience. We heard something of our colonel's record; how he had enlisted in the very first days of the war, leaving a lectureship at McGill, of his service in France and the wound he received in battle, following which he stayed with the battery, directing operations and refusing to go to the dressing station until the show was over.

Generally we referred to him as Andy. That is a mark in his favour. No general who was worth his salt was without a nickname. A host of illustrations occur to me: Ike, Monty, Old Blood and Guts, Papa Joffre, Black Jack and Bobs. I am not scholar enough to tell you what their men called Julius Caesar, Alexander and Hannibal, but I am soldier enough to know that it was not Caesar, Alexander or Hannibal. Add to the list of nicknames Corporal John, the Duke of Marlborough, who was idolized by his men and who, when the cares of command would permit, loved to leave his staff, fall in as a trooper and ride in a cavalry charge. He did that almost once too often at Malplaquet where, as Winston Churchill tells us in his life of his ancestor, in a clash with the French Household Cavalry he was unhorsed, overridden and barely escaped death. It was Marlborough's blood in the veins of his descendant that made Churchill demand, unsuccessfully, the privilege of landing with the troops in Normandy on D Day. We did not realize it at the time, but the fact that few of our generals had nicknames should have prepared us for the opinions we formed when later, after the war, we had a chance to read critical accounts of some of our campaigns.

Andy wore well. In France we found him even better than in England. When the first chilly nights came in September before we left Ypres for the Somme people began to think of artificial heat. One of the majors of our brigade had an elaborate stove made by the farrier's shops with draughts, dampers, a good door and stovepipes made of sheet iron. When it was delivered at the gun position some minor defect was discovered and it was returned to the horse lines for correction. The same day the colonel came out of his quarters at brigade headquarters, asked for an oil drum and, when one was produced, grabbed a pickaxe and punched some holes in its sides, making a brazier. Stories like that spread quickly and within twenty-four hours we had all heard about it.

A similar incident occurred at Doullens the first night of our march north from the Somme. The same major told his officers' cook that he wanted something good for dinner after a hard day's march. Who would not? He added that he wanted something nice for dessert. Long after the other officers had eaten the colonel turned up at the brigade mess. With four batteries in his charge he had not thought of his own needs until he had seen that everything possible had been done for man and beast. The cook asked what he wanted, expecting at least an order for bacon and eggs.

"Get me a tin of bully," said the colonel, "and some bread and a mug of tea."

We had not been on the road an hour the next morning when every man in the brigade had heard that story.

Late one night at the Somme the gunners in the pit next to mine made a pot of tea. A pot of tea at the front often cost the taxpayers a lot of money. A brazier with damp fuel was not a very satisfactory means of heating water. We had a method of making a quick mug of tea. We started with an eighteen-pounder shell, worth at least thirty 1916 dollars. We made sure that the propellant in the cartridge case was cordite, the grain charge was no good for our purpose. Then we loosened the shell from the case and removed the cordite sticks. Lighted and held by the end, with the flame under a tin of water, they had the water in a bubbling boil almost before the man with the tea can could get the lid off. Those midnight pots of tea tasted good even to a man like me who wished that they were coffee. They did not actually cost the taxpayer thirty dollars. There was some salvage; the shell case went back to be reloaded and the shell itself was very handy for paving muddy spots in the paths around the guns.

That night, as often, Andy was on the prowl. He was the darnedest man for wanting to know how things were going in his brigade. He came to the gun-pit where the tea was brewing and tried to get in. It was raining, as it usually was at the Somme, and the entrance to the gun-pit was covered with a rubber groundsheet. He had to crouch to get into the gun-pit and in so doing got tangled up in the groundsheet. Someone inside asked a perfectly natural question, "What the hell do you think you are doing with the groundsheet, you clumsy so-and-so?" The answer to that question was the colonel in person draped with the groundsheet. The sequel was very pleasant. The groundsheet was replaced with the help of the colonel. He then hopped upon a pile of shells and had a mug of tea with the boys. I do not recall any other officer sharing our mugs of tea.

I have my own private picture of our colonel. One night at the Somme there was a message from our battery to Brigade, something apparently that could not be sent by wire and had to be delivered that night. Somehow or other it turned out that I was the one who had to deliver it. I floundered around in the mud and finally reached Brigade. There I was told that the colonel was in bed and was instructed to take the message to him there. It was quite late, well after eleven o'clock, but when I reached the bottom of the stairs down to his dug-out I found him fully dressed and seated on his wooden bunk with his back against the planks of the wall, reading a book and surrounded by books. I had no chance to read their titles, but they looked like army textbooks of some kind. Here was our live wire relaxed and while relaxed preparing himself for the tasks still ahead.

Early in 1917 we lost our colonel. He left us to go to Corps as a brigadier in charge of counter-battery work. Sometime later that summer we heard that he had been killed while on a visit to the French Army. I well remember the shout that went up some weeks later when the transport driver came into the lines announcing, "Andy ain't dead; he was only wounded."

There was some controversy over our colonel after he became Minister of National Defence toward the end of World War II. I know where our boys stood on that argument. We old soldiers have few heroes but those we have we cherish jealously.

At the Somme I had buffer spring-case trouble. Old limber-gunners will understand that, no one else will care very much. That night the case and I went down the line in the ration wagon. By morning the spring-case was mended and ready to go back to its gun. Wagons could not go to that position in daylight and a man was detailed to go with me and help carry the spring-case. A wagon took us as far as Pozières where we were dumped out. The case was something under five feet in length and about six inches in diameter. A long pole was put through the middle of it, and we started off overland, well away from the road, with our burden on our shoulders.

It was a bright October morning with lots of sun, a most unusual thing for the Somme. The spring-case was made of some shiny white metal. As we topped the rise behind the battery we must have been visible half-way to Berlin. A German observer looking for targets of opportunity spotted us and must have been puzzled to name what he saw, but he had no doubt that it was something deserving his attention. And I must say for him that he was a good gunner. The first shell very nearly hit us. Fortunately there was an old trench nearby and before the third shell landed we were in it. The shelling kept up for some time, the German observer knowing that the shining object at which he was shooting was then in a shell hole or trench near where he had last seen it. Long before the shelling stopped someone joined us quite uninvited. He must have been running when he reached the trench and he did not look before he leaped. If he had looked I am sure he would not have landed on me, as he did, with both feet. He was a large, handsome, gray-haired person with a Scots cap, but no kilt, and the insignia of the Chaplain's Service on his uniform.

I regarded him coldly. A pair of Highlander's feet on the back of my neck would have been unwelcome even without the army boots. My resentment soon vanished when I realized that our visitor—I am sure it was he—was the Rev. Dr. Charles William Gordon, better known as Ralph Connor, a household word in Canada then, and still well remembered for his best-selling novels. He had been going down the line alone when he got caught in the shelling we had stirred up. When the shelling stopped he decided to go with us in spite of the fact that we were going in the direction from which he had just come. The Somme battlefield was no place for an elderly gentleman to be wandering around alone, even if his veins were full of Highland blood. Before starting out we hunted around in the trench and found a bundle of unused sandbags. We wrapped them around our shiny spring-case and made the rest of our way to the battery without any further attention from the German officer on the other side of the line, who about then, no doubt, was trying to decide what he should put in his record as to the nature of the target of opportunity on which he had expended some twenty shells.

At our gun-pit our guest perched himself upon a pile of shells and watched us re-assemble the gun. If I did not know that in his months with his Scots regiment from Winnipeg he had already heard it all, and more, I would be ashamed of some of the things he heard as we struggled to get that cantankerous gun together. Just as we finished the job a small party passed on the way to the rear. Our visitor joined them. That was the last I saw of the only VIP who ever jumped on me with both feet. Lots of officers did it from time to time but they did not do it physically.

In our early days in France we had a future VIP in our brigade although not in our battery. This was a person by the name of Smythe, since the war connected somewhat extensively with professional hockey. Some time early in 1917 he became fed up with the quiet life in the artillery and transferred to the Air Force. Before he left us he got permission to go over with the infantry on a trench raid. The way we heard the story there were no special duties for him to perform; he just went along on a sort of tourist's visa. In World War II he raised a battery and took it overseas. Just before the landing in Normandy he was told that he was too old for that young man's war and was relieved of his command. He went to headquarters about that and got his battery back. It was no doubt felt that anyone who could fight brass the way he did could fight Germans. Rumour says that the men he saw at headquarters did not get their breath back for two days.

Our foremost future VIP was a lieutenant named Massey. Before my time with the battery it was in training for some months in the summer and autumn of 1915 at Niagara Camp. Among the officers was a supernumerary attached only for training. He did not go overseas with us but did follow us later with another battery. He is, however, well and favourably remembered by such of our boys as were at Niagara Camp.

His first name was Raymond. When you hear his name now you think of Abraham Lincoln and Dr. Gillespie. That of course was long before he was known as anything but one of the Massey boys, the descendants of one of the founders of a great Canadian industry. I well remember the thrill we used to experience in France when we saw, as we often did, the name Massey-Harris on the side of a binder or mower.

Sanitary arrangements at Niagara Camp were rudimentary

in those days, and when the battery needed a bath some officer marched the men over to Lake Ontario where they stripped off on the beach and had a good swim. One day late in October the wind was blowing across the lines towards the officers' quarters, the major sniffed the breeze, announced that the battery needed a bath and detailed the super-numerary to conduct a bathing parade.

Lieutenant Massey marched the boys over to Lake Ontario. It was a coldish October day and the swim was short but invigorating. As the bathers came out of the water Massey could not repress a chuckle at their shivering plight. Without waiting to dress they seized him and threw him into Lake Ontario, uniform and all. The fact that that was done without reprisals is, I think, the best evidence that he was a regular guy.

10: For Strong Stomachs Only

I counted two-and-seventy stenches,
All well defined, and several stinks!
SAMUEL TAYLOR COLERIDGE

And therfor who-so list it nat to heere
Turne over the leefe and cheese another tale.
GEOFFREY CHAUCER

Much of what I have told you so far has been of pleasant things, things one enjoys recalling; little of it has its gruesome side. Even heavy fighting is not necessarily unpleasant. Some of the things I mean to tell of now can only be described as nauseating, and the reader who cannot bear to read such things is advised to turn to the next chapter. But I must go on. War is not the adventure one might think after reading some of my earlier chapters. I have pleasant memories of many things, but they are only part of the picture. What follows will give you some idea of the rest of it.

One of the pleasant pictures was our second position at Ypres. We were in a slight depression not far from the spot where General Mercer was killed on the morning of June second, 1916. The day after we took over the position the front was quiet and the scene was one of pastoral peace. Our guns were in the line of a hedge still partly in bloom. The meadows around us were filled with wildflowers and in parts almost red with poppies. On the crest in front there was a line of trees, still lovely to look at in spite of some telltale gaps and shattered trunks and branches. It had been a warm day, sunny and clear. And there was a sunset, a gentle pink and gold sunset, which seemed made for the scene. All that was lacking was the tinkling of a cowbell and the babbling of a brook. But there were no cowbells left tinkling around

Ypres, and brooks there did not babble; if they made a noise at all it was the gurgle of escaping marsh gas.

And, as befits a perfect summer evening, there was a little breeze, just enough to fan one's cheek, a wandering zephyr that came from the east and set the poppies nodding in the meadows around our guns; a gentle breeze with a faint, sweetish, sickish taint, the smell that comes from dead men after a few days, lying unburied beneath the summer sky.

That is what this chapter is about. Now turn to the next chapter.

Oddly enough, and fortunately, smells were not common, or if they were we got used to them. Places which should have smelled to high heaven were practically odourless. Our first position at the Somme was one of these.

It was a particularly untidy place. The word *untidy* does not refer to the mess that was typical of all battlefields but to the care, or lack of it, with which casualties had been removed. Our first position there was on the edge of the Sugar Trench in gun-pits that we took over from a battery being relieved. There had been heavy fighting for the Sugar Trench and after it was taken little was done to clean it up. We went in by daylight up a long valley in which, for a quarter of a mile at least, we were under direct observation. We made that quarter of a mile at a gallop and perhaps because of the haze we drew no fire. During that gallop one of our gunners lost his tin hat. As soon as we were in action he went to find a replacement. He did not have far to go. Not more than fifteen feet from the door of our gun-pit was a tin hat lying face down. When he picked it up he found a skull in it. Not ten feet from where the shrapnel helmet lay there was a partly buried infantryman. Someone had thrown a few shovelfuls of earth on him where he lay face down on the spot where he was killed. The earth was mostly on his body. His pack, part of his head, both his arms and most of his legs were quite uncovered. All along the approach to the trench there were semi-interments just like that. The

145

attackers who died approaching the trench were left where they fell, with a little earth thrown over them and not much more than half covered.

Our guns were just short of the trench and our first aiming post was set on the back of it. I well remember what I saw there the first evening when I went out to light the siege lamps; I had been busy on the dial sight when the posts were planted. When the trench had been reached there had been heavy hand-to-hand fighting. The casualties of both sides were still there, half buried, like the ones on the approach to the trench. There really should have been a stench there. I have forgotten how long we were in that position but it was probably two weeks. I am ashamed to record that in all that time we did practically nothing to clean up the mess.

It was there that one of Colonel McNaughton's orders was disobeyed or at least circumvented. When we took over that position the men in the gun-pit next to mine found that in digging the gun-pit their predecessors in occupancy had uncovered a German buried about two feet below the surface. When the pit was finished there was a German jackboot sticking out in one corner, just about splitting the angle and jutting out from a point an inch or two below the knee, and with the German's leg in the boot. You perhaps know enough about soldiers to realize that that knee boot was used as an article of furniture; bandoliers, gas masks, water bottles, all sorts of things were hung on it like a hatrack. When the colonel came to see how we were in our new quarters he saw the jackboot and did not like it.

"Dig that man out," he said, "and give him a decent burial."

When the colonel was gone the boys held a council of war. That order entailed a lot of useless work. They compromised. They dug back around the boot, snapped the leg off at the knee, filled the hole in with a sandbag, and gave the leg and foot "a decent burial" somewhere outside.

After we helped to take the Regina Trench we moved up to a position just short of the Albert-Bapaume Road, half-way between the sugar refinery and Martinpuich, and firing directly over Courcelette. There conditions were much better. We were not near any main trench and were not in a spot where there had been heavy casualties. There were, however, two things that belong to this chapter. One was a shoulder blade with arm attached, quite bare except for a scrap of sweater on the forearm. It lay around unattended to all the time we were there. The other was a Highlander's leg from the knee down with its boot and Scots sock still on it. That leg seemed bewitched. We had to pass it on our way to get water from the communal water tank established near our first position. As we passed along the path to the water tank we would always see the Highlander's leg, but never twice in the same place. It seemed to be a magnet for shellfire and, no matter how often it was hit, it moved up and down the path and never away from it. As we started our trips with our water cans we made little bets on the current location of that Highlander's shin.

Vimy Ridge was a clean battlefield. I had a tourist's trip over No Man's Land the day after we took the ridge and it was already cleaned up. Here and there we would see some infantryman's discarded web equipment beside a red stain on the ground, but that was all there was to tell the tale of the fighting. Vimy furnishes no material for this chapter. Even that ghastly road down the east face of the ridge was kept clean. If you made a trip in and out, the things you saw, and there were plenty of them, were cleaned up before you came back and replaced by other unpleasant sights.

Although the battlefield was clean there were gruesome incidents at Vimy for some of our boys. Ten of them were sent on a fatigue party to dig a pit for a trench-mortar battery that had been assigned the duty of demolishing a machine-gun nest just across No Man's Land on the morning of the attack. The spot selected for the pit was in the centre of a civilian cemetery. As the pit was ten feet deep it passed through many graves. French graves are often multiple with

147

as many as six layers. What came out was put in sandbags and deposited outside the pit. Before they finished there were many shin bones protruding and in one place part of a head with long flaxen hair. The boys used the shin bones as racks for their gas masks and canteens, and one of them made a point of combing and arranging the blonde hair.

Passchendaele was bad enough though not as bad as the Somme. There was a determined effort to clean it up but conditions made it difficult. By one German pillbox there was a pile of dead Germans that was there for at least three weeks after I first saw it. They were piled neatly like cordwood, four this way and four that, at least twelve feet long, and as high as the top of the pillbox.

We had standing orders at Passchendaele to take a flank if we were shelled, except at dawn or dusk when we might be needed to repel counterattacks. One day, in getting away, I saw a pair of German jackboots sticking up from the water in a large shell hole. The German, I judge, had been running and had tripped and fallen into the water where his hands had stuck in the mud at the bottom of the shell hole, trapping him and leaving his legs sticking straight up. The boots were new and I made a note of the place so that I could get them on the way back when the shelling had stopped. I found the place without trouble but I was too late; by the time I came back there was nothing to be seen but a pair of stockinged feet sticking up out of the water.

You have heard how our guns were pinpointed and shelled in our second position at Passchendaele. It was not practicable to move the guns but we did move our sleeping quarters to a flank. The ground was so bad that it was hard to find a path from our bivies to the guns, but we finally found a route that had only one really bad spot in it. Fortunately in the middle of that bad spot there was a dead German lying face down in the mud. All the time that we were there we used the seat of his pants as a stepping stone.

This chapter has been short even if it has not been sweet. I have been looking back over it and wondering if a man— or a boy, as I was—could have seen such sights and lived with them, as we did, without being coarsened and brutalized. I look at myself and I try to be objective. I believe that I can honestly say that, except for my vocabulary when I am annoyed, I think I am no worse than if I had never been to war.

11: Nights Out

The evil thing that walks by night.
JOHN MILTON

Much of the war took place in hours of darkness. Many things already told happened at night but some things stand out in my mind peculiarly as night scenes. They deserve, I think, a chapter by themselves.

On our arrival in France in July, 1916, we spent a few days near Steenvoorde, on the Ypres front. The weather was fine and we slept on the ground under our vehicles. It was not our first experience of sleeping under guns and wagons nor was it the last, though we soon became adept at finding shelter where there seemed to be none. The field we slept in near Steenvoorde was beside a main road. The third night we were there we were awakened about midnight by a band. Soldiers as well as civilians love bands. We rolled out of our blankets and slipped through the hedge onto the road. The band came by playing lustily, followed by a group of infantry not much more than twice the size of the band. Right by us they stopped for a breather, the infantry slipped out of their web equipment, sat on their kit-bags, and lighted the half-smoked fags they took from behind their ears. They were up from the Somme, they told us, out for rest and reinforcement.

We knew about the Somme, which had started a few days before we left England. There we had read about the splendid successes and the staggering blows to the enemy. Now we could get first-hand word of the battle. All they would tell us was that it was "bloody awful." Well might they say that. That little handful of men, barely more than twice the size of the band, was all that was left of a battalion that two short weeks before had been twelve hundred strong and the pride of the British Army. Soon their breather was over, they shouldered their packs, the band struck up again and they were on their way to rest billets where they would be reinforced and made ready for another battle. We were to learn more about the Somme shortly, and more directly, after a short apprenticeship at Ypres.

Our first gun position in France was on the edge of the moat at Ypres just outside the Menin Gate. That was a well-known spot in World War I. There were two swans in the moat and English illustrated papers published many pictures of them floating peacefully on the broad, deep water of the moat. For background they showed the immense mediaeval wall of the city and part of the city gate. Our gun position was just out of those pictures. It was not something that would have fitted into that peaceful scene. The whole embankment was a wilderness of shell holes and shattered trees. If you visit it today you see a wide boulevard, lined on the far side by lovely villas with lush green lawns and massive flower-beds.

A few nights after we went into action there, there was a bombardment, not of our position though we got some of that, too, but of the town. The shells were falling in a section where we knew that there was a Toronto battalion in reserve. I had already been under fire several times, I had seen a man killed and several wounded, but the sensation I got from those things was nothing like what I felt that night on the Ypres moat. The night was pitch-dark and we sat outside the gun-pits staring at the inky sky and listening to the great shells roaring overhead like aerial freight trains, to burst with a rending *crump* among our friends. If we had known then, as we soon knew, how much heavy shelling could be ineffective we would not have been so upset. But being green troops we were upset, more in fact than if we had been the target and not just sympathetic spectators. It was not long, however, before other people's troubles ceased to bother us.

Two of my night memories have to do with clouds of smoke from bursting shells floating across the sky; once against a clear moonlit sky, the other against a black backdrop with front lighting furnished by the flashes of six guns firing at the rate of four rounds per minute.

The first one was at Passchendaele late in November and long after we had taken the ridge and village. We had our guns in the most advanced position there, well forward so that we could reach deep behind the enemy lines with harassing fire, and where we could be more easily reached by return fire. Our gun flashes told the Germans that there was a battery in a new spot and they also told them just about where we were. To pinpoint us and save ammunition, a plane came over flying low, not more than a couple of hundred feet up, and directly over the centre of our battery shot out a signal, a bright flash, followed by a little cloud of smoke, which hung for a moment or two. We knew that other eyes than ours had seen that signal, eyes in two separate spots that measured angles and figured out our position to the breadth of a hand. Their detailed and accurate contour maps of a position that they had recently occupied gave our elevation accurately. We knew that we were as vulnerable as if we were out in the open with no cover at all.

That night and many nights thereafter we had very clear and cogent evidence that German gunners, though unimaginative in their firing, were accurate and persistent. We were on slightly higher and firmer ground in that position and had built bivies that would hold four men. One night we heard a cry for help following closely on the latest *crump*. I lay nearest to the door and was the first one out of our bivy and what I saw was not pleasant. The nearest bivy to ours, about twenty feet away, was without a roof and almost without walls. It had had a direct hit. In the mud some ten or twelve feet from the blasted bivy was a man on his hands and knees. It was his voice that we had heard calling for help. I paused beside him for a moment to see that he seemed to be in fair shape and then passed on to look into what had once been a bivy. One glance under the full moon told me that there was no one there who needed help. It was there next morning that we found the hand mentioned in my introduction, which now lies alone in France under a cross bearing a name and regimental number. We identified the hand by a ring.

I went back to the wounded man. He had been on guard and had been crouched on his heels talking to the men in the shelter when the shell landed. He told us that his leg hurt. Both his legs were buried in slime that reached a few inches above his knees. The mud came up his arms some inches above the wrists. The only wound that we could see was in his hip. There a fragment of a shell about two inches square was imbedded so that its surface was almost an inch below the flesh level. Oddly enough there was no haemorrhage. I stayed with him while the rest went for the stretcher. It was while they were gone that I saw the clouds of smoke. The next morning I was puzzled that my recollections were so fragmentary. I could remember kneeling beside the wounded man, with my arm around his shoulder, talking to him. I could not remember the roar of any approaching shells, nor the *crump* of their bursts. But I had a clear recollection of clouds of smoke passing between me and the moon, and very close.

It was only when I looked back on the scene that I realized that that smoke was from new shellbursts. I have no idea how many shells there were. There must have been a great many for one of the men who brought back the stretcher told me that, as they came back, they did not expect to find either the wounded man or me. But for me there were no shellbursts, only black clouds drifting across the moon.

We loaded the stretcher and carried it on our shoulders down the plank-road to the dressing station in the old German pillbox. I was at the front left corner of the stretcher.

From time to time I would say to the head a foot or so from mine, "You'll be OK, Len." Invariably the head replied, "I 'ope so, Hernie." At the dressing station we found why he had complained about his leg. When he was taken from the stretcher and the mud was removed from his leg it was found that one foot was practically severed. It was attached only by a shred of flesh. And again, astonishingly, there was no haemorrhage. And Len was OK. Until a few years ago he came to our reunions on his artificial foot.

My second recollection of flying shell smoke at night is equally vivid in my memory but not nearly so unpleasant. This time our guns were in action. On September twenty-seventh in the last year of the war we crossed the Canal du Nord in front of the Inchy and captured the Bourlon Wood. There was no flash-cover for us, for we went into action just over the crest and on the slope down to the canal east of Inchy. Lines were laid out for us and aiming-posts planted the afternoon of the twenty-sixth and we went into position during the night. The barrage opened in that dark hour just before dawn. We had not been in action very long when there was return fire. Having no flash-cover at all, our position could be calculated in a few minutes. We could not hear the shells approach nor hear them burst. In the rolling drumfire of an opening barrage you could not even hear your own gun. Our only knowledge of the bombardment, aside from casualties, was the sight of bursts and clouds of smoke floating around us. We saw them only momentarily in the flashes from our guns. The flash from a field gun is bright and sharp and illuminates everything for a considerable distance. In such an operation, to facilitate control, our guns had to be close together. With six guns firing four rounds a minute there was a flash on the average every two seconds. No shell-burst went unilluminated.

It was a weird and eerie scene. Our guns were in a well of inky blackness accentuated by the dazzling effect of the gun flashes. As each gun spoke there was a momentary glare in which the smoke from bursting shells was clearly seen, then for a second or two darkness again. I was better placed to see it than most. Each man had a job to do but, as sergeant, unless something went wrong I had nothing to do but time the shots and give the order to fire every fifteen seconds. That order was given by an upraised arm and a flashlight. With hundreds of guns roaring continuously orders had to be given visually.

My view of the scene was interrupted by a casualty. Number Two fell off the gun seat. Number Two set the range and, as the gun returned from the recoil, opened the breach. When Number Two hit the ground he grabbed his stomach with both hands and rolled around in obvious agony. I got his hands away with difficulty but could find no injury. Then we found his hand soaked with blood. Following that clue we found a hole in his sleeve about the size of a half-dollar. We got a field dressing on his arm and sent him away to the dressing station with envy in our hearts—a nice, cushy Blighty and a winter in England.

I ordered Number Six up on the gun seat. He put out his left arm to open the breach and then beckoned to me with his right hand. I went over to him and he shouted in my ear, "Put your light on my arm." I did. There in the same spot in the arm was an identical hole about the size of a half-dollar. Two men had received identical wounds in practically the same spot; one had rolled on the ground in agony and the other had not known that he was hit until he had tried to move his arm. The explanation is probably simple, but I am not the one to give it.

We were a lucky gun crew, two Blighties, a third of a crew, and no one really hurt. It had not always been a lucky gun. It was the gun that I had taken over, and ceased for the rest of the war to be the spare sergeant, when the gun crew was wiped out on the morning of August eighth. There are two matters of similarity between that affair and our barrage at Inchy. On the first morning of the Hundred Days our battery went into action in front of Hangard Wood without ranging and without flash-cover. Soon after the barrage started they were located and given a good going-over. One air burst caught B gun, my gun, squarely and wiped out the whole gun crew. At first it was thought that one of the men was not hit. He helped to carry one of the wounded men to the dressing station where, on arrival, he sat down for a rest. It was then he noticed for the first time that his boot was drenched with blood and that he had a nice piece in his leg. He did not take his Blighty as a soldier should. Instead of being delighted he was mad clear through. Before leaving for England and white sheets on his cot, he rushed out of the dressing station when he saw some German prisoners passing and punched one of them square on the nose. If that German is still living I imagine he is still wondering what that punch was all about.

There were two things that happened after dawn that morning in front of Bourlon Wood which, while they did not occur at night, might just as well come in here. The shelling of our battery did not last long. Our infantry and tanks advanced and the German guns were either captured or pulled back to avoid capture. After an early and hurried breakfast our horses came up and we moved forward. We crossed the Canal du Nord at a point where the plain was lower than most of the district and the canal was all above ground, the canal consisting of two great cement walls supported by earth embankments. The walls had been breeched and the canal drained. We did not go over the canal, we went through it on its dry bed.

As we came out on the other side there was a wide, grassy plain rising slightly toward Bourlon Wood. What we saw there made us catch our breath. That wide, sloping plain was dotted with little khaki mounds, all motionless, for the stretcher-bearers had already done their work. They were men of a Toronto battalion that had passed that way. Just a few hours before those khaki mounds had had a hasty breakfast and a good shot of rum and started off gamely to do something that they hoped might get them home before Christmas. I do not think a soldier ever gets too hardened to be affected by such a scene, specially if it is a battalion from his home town.

Half an hour later we saw something else. We were going up a depression, or gully, leading to Bourlon Wood. There we found a battery that had got there before us. Probably they had not been in the barrage at all or, at most, had fired a few rounds and then gone forward just behind the infantry to take on targets of opportunity and destroy strong points. There they had run into a German field battery that had not yet been captured and whose gunners no doubt were cursing the drivers who had not yet come up to pull them out. The marching battery was in column of route, single file, six guns and six wagons, twelve vehicles in all. The Germans had them in open sights at a very short range. There had been no time, apparently, to get even one gun in action. I do not say that the whole battery was there and that none had escaped; we did not count the vehicles as we passed, noting only that the stretchers had already been there and there was no need for help. I will not try to describe it except to say that it was one jumbled mass of shattered guns and wagons mixed with bodies of men and horses. I hope that German battery did not get away.

That was September twenty-seventh. The next day Ludendorf sent an urgent demand to Hindenburg to arrange an armistice. Twenty-five years later to the day I was dressed up in khaki again, giving gun drill to the Veterans' Guard unit I was connected with during World War II, when during a break for a smoke our major looked at his watch.

"What do you suppose," he asked me, "I was doing twenty-five years ago today?"

I thought a moment. "Bourlon Wood," I said.

"At this moment by my watch, not allowing for difference in time, I was cutting off the rest of my arm with a penknife."

The arm was only a small part of the injuries he sustained. Sometimes the Veterans' Guard went out for a march on the city streets just to show what real soldiers look like. We were

157

very proud of our Fragment from France stepping along ahead of us with his empty sleeve blowing in the wind.

A few nights later we had another night action. We had passed Bourlon Wood and were closing in on Cambrai. Some strong point was giving trouble and the line had to be strengthened. There was a limited operation just at dusk and we formed part of the group that supplied the barrage. After the line was straightened we lifted our range and until after eleven o'clock each gun fired one round a minute to discourage any ideas of counterattack. It was then that the fun started. We were in the open. The last gun-pits we saw in France were those granite and railway-tie beauties we had built at the Arras station. As soon as we went into action the German Air Force was called on for assistance. Night bombing of the rear lines had been fairly common for some time but that was the first time that we ever had an organized bombing raid on the guns.

Those bombers must have had a lot of fun. They came over in a continuous stream, one at a time, circled around over the gun positions and, when a gun fired, tried to hit the spot where they had seen the flash. Some of their tries were pretty good and, while they had no way of knowing how close they came, they must have had quite a time. We had our own defensive tactics, made possible by the round-a-minute rate of fire. We would fire, reload and relay as quickly as possible and then lie flat on the ground, getting as much cover as we could from the gun and ammunition wagon, and wait for the rest of the sixty seconds to elapse until we fired again. We did that for four hours, at the end of which time we got the order *Cease fire*, and the bombers lost their target. One bomb had landed in front of my gun, about ten feet from the muzzle. The gun next to mine had been hit but not put out of action. Half of the bullet-proof shield had been torn away by a bomb that landed just in front of it, and two gunners had acquired fine Blighties. The gunners with that ruined shield were as proud of it as we Veterans' Guard men were

158

of our one-armed major and hated to relinquish it for a trip to Ordnance workshop when a replacement was available. A busted gun on the road gave one as much distinction as a gold wound stripe on the arm.

We were lucky that the Germans had been using ordinary percussion bombs and not their new spring-bombs. Rumour said that those spring-bombs had a rifle cartridge in the nose, which exploded on contact, then threw the bomb back twenty or thirty feet into the air, where it exploded. They were filled with nuts and bolts, washers, worn-out ball bearings, and other discarded hardware. Properly placed they could be devastating to troops and animals in the open. One of our division horse lines was plastered with them and hardly a horse was not hit.

After we stood down we had to do something about sleeping. We were not unused to rolling up in our blankets around the guns but, with bombers around, we wanted some protection. My gun crew slept in the bomb hole in front of our gun. We unstrapped the shovel, carried on the gun, and squared off the bottom of the hole, making a good level space where all six of us slept comfortably. Usually in that open warfare of the last few months, if there were no shell or bomb holes to start with, we slept in slit-trenches. Each man dug a hole about the size of his body and lay down in that. How deep you went depended on how lazy or tired you were and how much you depended on your luck. After the spring-bombs turned up we all went pretty deep.

Not all of my night memories are unpleasant. I have told you of our night march to Vaux-en-Amienois to have our guns tested for muzzle velocity. *En route* we passed through Amiens. The great city was nearly deserted, and those who had stayed were wrapped in slumber. There it lay, white and dead, flooded by the light of a full moon. As we passed along one of the avenues our view was obstructed by a high stone wall. In the middle of the wall was a large gap, the handiwork of some stray shell or bomb. Through the gap we saw a fine mansion set in a large garden in full bloom. I dismounted and, being the only outrider in the party, handed my reins to the lead driver of the first gun. Then I darted through the gap. I had only a moment or two to take in the scene. Presently I plucked a large, fragrant rose, spread it carefully and put it in my pay book. Then I ran after my party and remounted. In my next letter home I sent the rose, which had been well pressed in my pay book in my tunic pocket. I still have that rose, its condition remarkably good after more than forty years, and sometimes I look at it and try to recapture the beauty of that moonlit garden.

There was very little beauty in that world of mud and lice and death. When we encountered it we remembered it. One such scene was on a night march from Ablain-St. Nazaire to Vimy, when we were preparing to take the ridge. On the road we saw an air raid somewhere in the rear. Judging by the number of searchlights the raid must have been on one of the ports. It was so far away that we could not hear the bursting bombs or the firing archies. All we could see was the searchlights, those probing fingers of light in the inky sky, searching, searching until they found what they sought and then staying on it, in a cone, for the archies—the anti-aircraft guns—to do their work.

Archies never impressed us as being very scientific or effective. Often it was impossible to locate the airplane target by watching the archie bursts. I was credibly informed by a member of a Canadian anti-aircraft battery that its total score for the war was three planes, and that one of those three planes was shot down while the battery was being fired by a lieutenant who is now an eminent judge. There were two German planes in sight, says my friend, about three miles apart. While firing at one plane the battery brought down the other. That reminds me of another judge who, as a student, was a member of the Osgoode Hall Rifle Association in the early days of the war and while firing on the rifle range at Long Branch scored a bull's-eye on target eight with a shot directed at target nine.

We always enjoyed the archie shoots. They broke the monotony, which was often one of our worst problems. We watched them with interest and were their ardent fans, even though they never seemed to hit anything. We would stand in the open with shrapnel dropping all around us just to watch them. There was a curious belief that archie shrapnel was harmless by the time it got down to us. Oddly enough I never heard of anybody being hit by it. The only casualty of that kind was one of our boys who got a nice Blighty when a machine-gun bullet hit him in the leg while he was watching an air dogfight.

Trench raids were usually welcomed by the artillery as breaks in the monotony. We enjoyed them, but I am not so sure that the infantry did. Particularly interesting were raids on a flank, which left one free to watch if, as sometimes happened, we were in a position where we could see the show. There was a raid like that one night, when we were at Vimy village, on a powerhouse that was the scene of frequent local scraps. It was an early raid, after sundown and before midnight. It was the noise that drew our attention to what was afoot. We were out of our cellars in a moment and were surprised to find that we had a perfect grandstand seat. First there were Very lights, those great glaring rockets that lit up No Man's Land like daylight. There were SOS signals, usually red rockets. The sky seemed to be full of them. There were other rockets, red, yellow and blue, each one telling its own tale to someone in the rear. Mingled with this were scores of bursting shells, the shrapnel flashing like sparklers at a fireworks display and the HE sending up clouds of smoke that presently billowed through the glare of the Very lights. Presently the noise and the fireworks died down. Then we knew that there would be roll-calls and the stretcher-bearers would be at work.

161

In spite of what it meant in blood it was always pleasant to listen to and watch someone else's scrap. That sudden roar of gunfire and the *rat-tat-tatting* of machine-guns on our flank always gave us a thrill. I have often wondered what our gunfire in a big barrage must have sounded like behind the lines. Only once did I have a chance to hear anything like it and that was only a minor do, a push for the Pimple, which was not taken on the morning we took the ridge, but was taken a few days later. I was out at Ordnance workshop with my gun, which had been hit on our first night in Vimy village. I was in my bunk at the opening of the barrage, some ten or fifteen miles away, and lay there enjoying it until it was time to get up. That was only a taste, a sip; I never had the full drink. The barrages at the Somme, Vimy Ridge and Ypres heard from ten miles must have been out of this world. I recall reading that Lloyd George went out on the Downs near Dover during the Somme where, though he could not hear a sound, he could feel with his feet the vibration of the bombardment that was carried in the great chalk bed beneath the topsoil all those hundred and thirty odd miles from the battlefield.

One German raid on our front caught us unprepared. The rest of the gun crew were in the next gun-pit playing poker. It was a hot August night and I had retired, lying on top of the blankets on my bunk in my birthday suit, when a signaller stuck his head out of the control-pit shouting, "SOS". I was beside the gun in less time than it takes to write the words. The gun was loaded and laid on our SOS line, and all I had to do was pull the firing lever to put an air-burst just in front of our trench where raiders might be approaching it. I fired, reloaded and fired a second round before any other gun on our front spoke. By that time the other gunners were in the pit and I got some clothes on.

We gunners had nothing to do with the Very lights. The nearest we ever came to them was when we saw them high in the sky a mile or so away. With my knack for getting tangled

162

up with things that were not my business, I managed to have an experience with one of them. After we had been in Vimy village for some weeks I was sent down to the horse lines for a few days. I decided to walk down and have my blankets and kit come out on the ration wagon. I got to the wagon lines after dark and was met with the unpleasant news that there had been a casualty at the guns and I was to go back at once. The ration wagon had just left so I decided to go back overland. That way I would beat the ration wagon to the guns and be sure that my blankets and kit would stay where I needed them. I went over the old trenches and climbed the ridge to the left of the Arras-Lens road, just about where the Canadian Memorial now stands.

It was there that I met my Very light. Part of what I now say is based on surmise; I never did find out exactly what happened but imagine that someone had found a flare-pistol and had decided to try it out. He could not see me and I could not see him, but his aim could not have been much better if he had been using a peep-sight and it had been mid-day. Fortunately, while the line was perfect, it was a little high. I heard a *pop* and then fifty or a hundred feet away from me the flare burst into full incandescence and came apparently straight at me like a comet. It passed a few feet over my head. What happened to it after it passed me I have no idea, though probably it made a beautiful ricochet when it landed. It was seconds before I could move a muscle. If the joker who fired that flare ever reads these lines I hope that he realizes that he took five years off my life that night on the site of the Vimy Memorial. It is the unexpected and unknown that terrifies. I was still out of breath when I reached my cellar home in the village just in time to prevent my kit from going down on the ration wagon.

On the night of August sixth, two days before we started the Amiens push, I had to take up the rations. Our ammunition was all in and this was the last trip before the attack; nothing routine was to use the roads on the night of the

163

seventh. I had to go through Boves and, as might be expected, there was a beautiful traffic jam. It was the assembly point for a brigade of infantry. As the four battalions came up they were placed in the field on the four corners. There they stood easy and waited for further orders. It was some hours later that they left to go into hiding in the woods behind the front to wait for zero hour. I know it was some hours because I spent two or three hours waiting to get across that corner with my transport wagon.

Do you wonder how those boys spent the time waiting to move into the line? They knew that there was a big push coming and that the kick-off could not be much more than twenty-four hours away. Most of them had been in a push before and, from memories of the Somme, Vimy Ridge and Passchendaele, knew just what a push could mean for them. They had no way of guessing that this was going to be something quite unlike anything that they had done before and that within thirty-six hours they would, in places, be twelve miles behind the German lines, capturing generals in their dug-outs and a hospital train standing in a station loading casualties. How were they to know that they were only two days away from winning for the Canadian Corps the designation, by Marshal Foch, of "spearhead of the Allied Armies," and that in the Hundred Days, then starting, they would justify it well?

They could not think of those things and it was not a time for any thoughts. The boys at that crossroad had a singsong. Have you ever heard five thousand men in the open sing some of the old favourites? Even the drivers on my ration wagon joined. Not all the favourites, however. Songs like "There's a Long, Long Trail" were taboo. They were all gay ones, rollicking and sometimes rather bawdy. Once only, in a little lull, someone broke the unwritten rule. He started "I'll Take the Highroad." From across the road a hundred yards away from the singer came a voice, the voice of a man with a knife in his vitals: "Oh, for Christ's sake, don't sing that." Someone had been thinking of his true love. That was why thoughts

164

before a battle were a bad business. Thoughts might easily turn to folks at home who, on balance, though they had not so much to lose, might have more to bear than we.

Eventually we got through the jam and reached the battery in time to come back just as it was breaking dawn. As we came back we found the fields filled with tanks, more than I ever saw together at any time before or since. They had come in overnight, the sound of their motors drowned out by the drone of airplane motors overhead. All night long a stream of bombers had passed back and forth, unloading their cargoes on targets so far behind the line that they were not easily identifiable as being on our front. That was only one of the many devices employed to prevent the enemy from guessing that we were massing on that front. Now the tanks were going to bed, some pulled into woods or clumps of bushes but most of them bedded down in the open fields. Each tank carried a giant fish-net camouflage. That was just what it sounds like, a great fish-net with irregular strips of canvas on it and loose pieces of canvas dangling down. That broke the lines and killed the shadows so that from the air and from any real distance those tanks were practically invisible; none of them was spotted on the day before the push.

I shall close this chapter with something frivolous. During the open warfare of the last months of the war the field artillery was handled in waves. Some of the batteries pulled out after the opening barrage and followed on the heels of the infantry, as we did on the second day of the Amiens push. Others were held back to provide the creeping barrage for further advance and to repel counterattacks. On the morning of August eighth we were held back. Before noon we were out of action, for those foot-sloggers had already got beyond our range. During the afternoon we moved across the old German trenches and stood for some time in the fields near the village of Demuin awaiting further orders.

Shortly after dusk we got the order to advance. That meant passing through Demuin. The streets of the village were narrow and there was another beautiful traffic jam. For a long time we stood in the centre of the town while four lanes of traffic tried to use a two-lane street. To the right of us was a battalion of infantry also stalled and mostly on the sidewalk. It was pitch-dark and one of the men decided this was the opportunity he had sought for long. He addressed himself to his platoon commander. I will not report what he said. Old soldiers can supply the words, young people would not understand them and I do not wish to corrupt the typesetter. What was said may be summarized as descriptive: the officer's ancestry, his appearance, including his ears, his personal habits and morals; all of these were discussed and commented on. The speaker must have been an old sweat; no draftee or remount could have acquired that complete army vocabulary in a short period of service.

The officer resented the remarks and tried to locate the offender. He would rush toward the voice shouting, "Stop that man! Hold that man!" The voice would be silent, only to break out again at the other end of the platoon. The uproar continued during nearly all the time that we were standing there. There were two things that make me feel that perhaps the officer had it coming to him. One is the fact that not one man apparently made any effort to stop the culprit; the other is that any good officer who had been with the platoon long enough to arouse that amount of enmity should have recognized the voice of any man in his platoon. Perhaps he was of the type, very, very rare, who were shot in the back, despite the fact that they never turned their backs on the enemy.

12: Going on Leave

The soldier's earthly Paradise.
HANS JAKOB CHRISTOFFEL VON GRIMMELSHAUSEN

You are probably not familiar with the writings of Hans Jakob. Neither am I. I stumbled on the extract from which the above line is taken. Hans Jakob lived over three hundred years ago and the extract is taken from his account of the foot soldiers in the Thirty Years War. Soldiers of all ages apparently have much in common. The paradise referred to was not leave but winter quarters, the nearest thing the soldiers of his day had to leave. Leave was a very important thing in our lives at the front, ranking next, and a close second, to eats.

The first leave pass to come to our outfit came unexpectedly and long before leave generally was due, which was not until we had been twelve months in the lines. One day an order came to the battery from Brigade to supply one general-service wagon, one sergeant and a number of men. That looked like an unpleasant chore and the sergeant who, as brigade orderly-sergeant, had helped to pluck stolen chickens was detailed for the job. Colonel McNaughton gave the instructions personally to the sergeant. He was to proceed to X where there was an abandoned brewery. There he was to load a boiler on the wagon and then transport it to Y where the colonel was having a bathhouse built. On arrival at the brewery, the sergeant looked the situation over and decided that the task was impossible. Somehow he managed to get a line through to Brigade and reported to that effect.

167

"Sergeant," said the colonel, "I did not send you to make a report. I sent you to do a job. Don't let me hear from you again until it is done."

With that kind of order there was nothing to do but do the job. That was one thing about our colonel, and one of the things that fitted him to command the Canadian Army in World War II, men could do the impossible for him. When the impossible had been completed the sergeant reported back to brigade.

"Where would you like to go on leave?" asked the colonel.

When he got his breath back the sergeant said, "London, sir," and that is where he went, on a ten-day pass, six months before any of the rest of us went on leave. When he reported back to our battery from the chore at Brigade, he asked the major casually, "Is there anything I can get for you in London, sir?" "Huh!" said the major. When he saw the pass he was almost in tears. Most of us would have given a foot for that scrap of paper.

One of our men almost never had a leave during his whole two and a half years at the front. His passes came in regularly but he always did his best to nullify them. His first pass came on the Vimy front and in due course he rode to the railhead station near Aubigny. A friend accompanied him to take back his horse. On arrival at the station they found that they were too early for the train and finding a nearby *estaminet* open they put their time to good use. When they returned to the station they made a nuisance of themselves, singing and talking with loud voices and some choice army vocabulary. The stationmaster, the RTO in army language, was an Imperial with an empty sleeve and Mons Star. He came over to them and told them to be quiet. The man with the pass resented that. He pulled himself up and beat his breast with his fist.

"I'm a fighting man," he said. "I don't have to take that from any — bomb-proofer living."

True enough, RTO was a bomb-proof job in those days before night bombing; but the empty sleeve and the Mons Star had passed unnoticed in the alcoholic haze. No man who could stand without holding onto something would think of addressing an officer, particularly an Imperial, in that manner, especially with a leave pass in his pocket that might be in jeopardy. Spectators expected to see the sky fall. What did that old soldier, the pre-war regular with the Mons Star, do? He was a real gentleman and not one by the terms of his commission only. He turned on his heel and walked away. A real bomb-proofer would have had the culprit in the clink with a cancelled pass.

The next pass for that man came shortly after Passchendaele, while we had horse lines near Neuville St. Vaast. Knowing that his name was high on the leave list and that leaves were generous after Passchendaele, he went out one night to celebrate. Where he got the liquor I do not know but I do know that he got much more than was good for him. On his way back to our lines, very late, he had to pass a forward casualty station commanded by a peppery old colonel with a sweeping white moustache and a burning face to vouch for his life in the Medical Corps in India. He was annoyed by the singing and came out of his quarters to protest. Again our gunner pulled himself up and pounded his chest with his fist.

"I'm a fighting man," he said. "And I don't have to take that from any — — — bomb-proofer living." You will note that there are two more blanks before the word bomb-proofer than there were the first time. His earlier success had gone to his head.

He was one of my gun crew. The next morning after the nine o'clock parade the major sent for me. The expected leave warrant had come in that morning and word had also been received that my gunner was in clink awaiting trial by court martial on charges covering almost everything but desertion and high treason.

"He's your man," said the major. "You get him out."

Just like that. *You get him out.* Not a word about the old colonel with the white moustache, who no doubt had his heart set on seeing my gunner spend the rest of his army days tied to a gun-wheel. Moving a brewery boiler must surely have been an easier task than the one assigned to me. I saddled up and was on my way. I must have ridden twenty miles that day. I have quite forgotten the number of officers I had to see but I do remember that each time I got a signature I was told that someone else had to sign, someone four or five miles back in the direction from which I had just come. The first officer I saw told me that nothing could be done without the consent of the colonel who had laid the charges. That interview was an experience to remember. I can still see that handlebar moustache working up and down his face, trying to keep pace with the emotions of a veteran with a generation of service in the tropics and with veins full of curry powder instead of blood. It was Passchendaele, I think, which turned the trick. The whole army by that time knew that story and no one would know it better than a Medical Corps colonel. Eventually I got his consent, accompanied by grumbling remarks about "bally colonials" and military discipline. The rest of the chore was comparatively easy, a simple matter of riding all day to get proper signatures.

It was nearly six o'clock and quite dark before I had acquired all the necessary signatures and arrived at the Monastery at St. Eloi, where my man was held in durance vile. Readers who lived through the first war will remember that monastery and its tower. The tower shared with the swans in the Ypres moat and the hanging figure on the church at Albert the honour of being the most photographed objects on the British front.

When I got to the monastery door that winter evening I was more than a little peeved at the gunner who had put me to so much trouble. Presently I saw a sight that assuaged my spirits. After my documents had been scrutinized and

170

accepted I was led down two or three flights of stone steps into the bowels of the earth. There I was shown a cell, which probably for hundreds of years had been used as discipline for refractory monks and sometimes, too, for offending peasants. There was a thick wooden door blackened by age. About face-high there was an opening in the door, an oblong about twelve inches by eighteen inches. Small as it was, it had two iron bars upright in it set solidly in the wood. The cell itself was about twelve feet by eight and, surprisingly, there was a fireplace in it in which, more surprisingly, there was a fire about the size of a man's hand.

On a stone bench in front of the fire and with his back to the stone wall sat my gunner, a picture of woe. His elbows were on his knees and his head was in his hands. He was staring gloomily into that spark of fire. He told me afterwards that some sadistic guard had told him that his leave warrant had come and that he probably would never see it because he was likely to be shot. With a hangover that blurred badly the occurrences of the night before he was not sure that that might not be the result. I was just mad enough and mean enough to stand there at the cell door and gloat over him for a full two minutes before I called to him. I know what a warden sees when he brings a pardon to a man in a death cell.

My first leave was in August, 1917, after more than thirteen months at the front. I remember telling that to an American soldier in front of the Eiffel Tower in Paris. As I stood gazing up at the Tower, he kept circling me, taking me all in: the pipe-clayed gunner's lanyard I had put on for leave, my leather bandolier well polished with even the brass fasteners brassoed; my two blue service chevrons, one for each year, the second one put up as soon as the second year started; my riding breeches and spurs, which had not yet lost their rowels. After he had taken me all in he stopped in front of me. "You been to the front?" he asked. I told him, yes. "How long?" he asked. I told him. He was struck with astonishment. "And you ain't dead yet," he said.

My first leave was shared with one of my drivers for whom it was his only leave. He was the Speedy that I mentioned in my introduction. In civil life he had been an hostler in a livery stable. In Paris he displayed an unexpected susceptibility to beauty. I can see him yet, standing in the Hôtel des Invalides looking down at the tomb of Napoleon, almost breathless with the emotion that that miracle of colour and lighting evoked. He was with me when I got into the Chamber of Deputies. There were four of us together, and seeing a guard we applied at the guardhouse. After some debate one of the guards conducted us across the square to the main entrance, where he turned us over to a most imposing individual. He wore a tricorn hat, knee breeches and silk stockings. On his shoes were large silver buckles and there was a heavy silver chain around his neck, which came down in several loops to his belt line. I was never quite able to decide if he was the head porter or the equivalent of the gentleman usher, Black Rod himself. When we left him we were in great perplexity trying to decide whether he was the kind of person one could, should or dare tip. We debated it aside and then it was put up to me to find out. I turned to him with a gesture toward my pocket and asked if it would be permissible. The smile and the sweeping gesture with which he deprecated the idea makes me think that probably he was the gentleman usher. Few people in France scorn a tip.

The last thing we saw there was the chapel attached to the Palais Bourbon, which in due course was converted into the Chamber of Deputies. We viewed it from a gallery. Not many people would say that it is one of the most beautiful chapels in the world, but to soldiers fresh from the filth of the battlefields it was breath-taking. For a moment Speedy stood motionless and then started saying in a half-whisper, "Jesus Christ. Jesus Christ." There was nothing either religious or irreligious in those words; they were simply the expression in army idiom of his deep emotion in the presence of beauty. Seldom have I met a man who was so deeply moved by beauty as that little hostler from the livery stable who, a few months later, smothered in the mud of Passchendaele.

My second leave came on the evening of March twentieth, 1918. That pass had the word *Rome* written on it. Rome leave was not often granted and I had been one of the lucky few. The major told me when he gave me my pass that I could go down the line that night or wait until the morning. We were in a quiet reserve position on top of the right flank of the ridge, firing over Farbus. There we were defending in depth waiting for the expected German push, sparked by men released from the Russian front. We had good dug-outs and I had a nice comfortable bunk. I decided to stay there overnight.

About three-thirty the guard came into our dug-out and shook me by the shoulder. "Listen to that, you damn fool," he said. "Now don't you wish you had gone down last night?"

By that time it was March twenty-first. That may not mean much to you. It was the day that the Germans made their last great push, the one that almost separated the French and British Armies and came close, for the last time in that war, to taking Paris. We were not on the front of the attack but were very close to its north flank. As flank cover the shelling was quite brisk. As soon as I had had my breakfast I started for Rome, via the horse lines, Aubigny and Paris. Passing through the rear line of an army under attack and at the moment in mortal peril, our progress was slow. It was late, almost midnight, when we reached Paris. Then we were told that there was an air raid in progress and were advised to get to our hotels as soon as possible. The streets were deserted except for fire-engines patrolling with screaming sirens. The sky was full of searchlights but no archies were firing. At intervals there would be a loud *crump,* but nothing landed in my vicinity. That was in the days of Zeppelins. On my first leave I had heard the sirens and the racing fire-engines and had heard the word *Zeppelin* hissed through teeth that chattered.

In the morning the air raid was still on but the scene was entirely different. What a difference daylight makes! The night before no one was to be seen in the streets; they were all indoors, most of them in their cellars. In the morning sunlight the streets were jammed with people walking, as I was, with craned necks, trying to see the Zeppelins or Gothas that were causing those periodic *crumps*. I walked for hours and saw nothing. For days afterwards I had a stiff neck. It was not until we saw the noon papers that we found out what the "air raid" really was. I had landed in Paris very soon after the first Big Bertha had landed, fired by the great gun more than eighty miles away. When the damage was inspected Paris laughed.

There was no laughter on Easter Sunday when one of the great shells hit an arch of the Madeleine church and toppled the masonry into the worshipping congregation, but generally speaking Big Bertha was a joke. I saw where one shell had hit a corner of one of the buildings of the Sorbonne. There were a few broken windows and that was all that one could see from the outside. I saw where one landed in the Place de la Republique. There were some shattered paving stones and a splinter had made a dent in the bronze statue of the Republique in the centre of the square. When I was there last I tried to find that dent in the bronze, but someone had repaired the statue's war wound. Parisians would look at the damage done by Big Bertha and then think of some scene, such as I saw in the Faubourg Montmartre, where an aerial torpedo dropped by a Gotha had hit a four-storey stone building and demolished it. The Frenchman would shrug his shoulders and be glad that it was a Big Bertha and not a Zep or a Gotha.

It was obvious to me almost at once that because of the push leave would be cancelled. That posed a question—the

174

kind of question that is its own answer. Should I spend the rest of that fast-deteriorating leave on the Rome express where I would be a sitting duck for every redcap looking for leave passes to cancel, or should I stay right there in Paris where there was room for manoeuvre and where any redcap who tagged me would have to be very alert and active? For four days four of us travelled in a group. At every corner one of us stepped forward and peeked around cautiously to see if any redcaps were in sight. If none was visible we all turned the corner. If one could be seen we retreated, or rather executed a strategic withdrawal.

Finally we were caught. The redcap took our pay books, put the date and the words *warned for the front* after the last entry of pay, and told us that we had to be out of Paris by nine o'clock the next morning. That gave us time to pick up our kit, if we knew where it was. Our passes were marked in the same way. Being caught in Paris after that deadline would have resulted in a charge of desertion. First we ascertained that there was a train going our way the next morning just before our deadline. Then we made our plans. There was a little wine shop on Rue Cambon, near the south end of the street and just around the corner from the Place de la Concorde. It was operated by a widow known to most Canadians on leave in Paris as Madame Louise. Behind the wine shop was a little restaurant, four or five tables at the most. When I was there a few years ago that wine shop had been turned into a bookstore.

We went there first, to order our last dinner in Paris. There was some sort of opinion in our group that I had more facility in the French language than the others. So I did the ordering. The result would seem to indicate that, while my command of French might be more than the others', it was not great. With dinner ordered we spent the rest of the day taking a last look at Paris. In due time we were back in the Rue Cambon for our dinner.

In the café was an old Frenchman who, when he heard that we were leaving for the front in the morning, insisted on

175

buying us cocktails. Not only did he buy them but he mixed them. He went behind the bar and produced what he called a *Sheecago* cocktail. When that was disposed of we proceeded with our meal. First came the oysters on the half shell. I had ordered a dozen for the four of us. What my French produced was a dozen for each of us. Then we had a salad, followed by soup. About that time the wine appeared. My quart bottle of sherry appeared as a quart bottle for each of us. No one complained—we did not want to hurt Madame Louise's feelings. Next we had fish, and a fairly large piece of it. Then came the main dish and it was exactly as ordered, two whole roast chickens, good-sized birds, full-grown but not mature, with dressing, roast potatoes and peas. All we left of those birds were the necks. For our first dessert we had preserved peaches, the second was French pastries. After our coffee we paid the bill—thirty-seven francs, seven dollars and forty cents. Madame Louise did not make much on that meal. After the bill was paid she brought in four napkins with liqueur glasses hidden in them. It was against the law to serve liqueurs to men in uniform. Each of those glasses contained a good jolt of chartreuse. I often think of that meal and wonder how even soldiers could get it all down. Perhaps the cocktails and the four bottles of sherry answer the question.

My third leave came in August just before we moved back from Amiens to the Vimy front. It was a special seven-day pass to compensate for my bobtailed leave in March. We were near Roye when the pass came. Another man went with me. We travelled first to Boves, where our horse lines had been when the push started, but which was then the railhead. There we found that there was no train until the following morning. For the first time since my March leave I slept in a real bed. That statement requires some qualification and explanation. Most of the village was deserted, so we looked around and found a large, likely looking house to sleep in. It was empty but much of the furniture was still there, the kind of things that a soldier could not carry away to furnish his quarters. In one of the upstairs rooms was a handsome bed. The only thing wrong with it was that the springs, mattress and bedding had already been removed. That did not faze us. We lay down on the floor without blankets inside the frame of the bedstead and slept, if not actually in a bed, inside a bed. Many a night since I have wished that I could sleep as I did that night on the hard floor with my haversack for a pillow.

Men going on leave always had a big send-off. Shined and polished as if for inspection by the King, you mounted and rode away accompanied by a horse-holder to bring your horse back to the lines. As you rode away you were followed by a little cheer. There was more envy than enthusiasm in those cheers. A man coming back sometimes got a cheer, too, especially if his face showed that his time had been well spent and that he was in the throes of a hangover.

It was always a special occasion when one of our bombardiers went on leave. He was our champion souvenir-hunter. Most of us had a touch of the disease but with Dinny it was a mania. When I saw his collection after we got home I could hardly believe my eyes. He had a whole German machine-gun, smuggled out in pieces. He had a suit of body armour that German snipers sometimes wore, which he must have worn under his uniform when he went on one of his leaves. When Dinny died he left his collection to his home town where it is now on display in glass cases in the town high school. His difficulty in getting his souvenirs home was that a good part of them were contraband. The stuff could be mailed or expressed from England but censorship would have stopped it if sent from France. Everyone going on leave to England had to take something for Dinny. When he went himself he was like a travelling arsenal. Once it took two men to get him on his horse; that was probably the time he took the body armour.

177

I had three leaves after armistice, two to Brussels and the other to London. Our last position at Grez-Doiceau was so close to Brussels that, with nothing useful to do except keep the horses alive, it was natural that short leaves should be frequent. The passes were for forty-eight hours and we got fifty francs from the paymaster to defray our expenses. As will appear presently that sum was quite inadequate. Our lodgings in the leave centre were free but we had to buy our meals and drinks. One of our boys spent two hundred francs the first night he was there trying to get drunk and gave up in disgust. The only drinks we could buy were Belgian beer, which no Anglo-Saxon would use for anything but washing a dog, and a liquor which we knew by the name of Schiedam. It was a colourless liquor that we took to be gin, but was so weak that it was hard to say what it was. We swore that what we got for our money was a glass of water in which some one had dipped the cork of a gin bottle. Food was rationed and food prices frozen, but prices of other things were exorbitant. A dish of sherbert in the Café Madrid cost five francs, one dollar according to our pay books. One day I saw some chocolates in a store window. They were the little round-pointed chocolates filled with a mixture that seemed to contain a percentage of chalk, which in Canada at that time cost about twenty cents a pound. The thought of a good candy feed appealed to me. I walked in and planked down a five-franc note. What I got was a little screw of newspaper with some candies inside. Out on the sidewalk again I opened the little package and counted the candies. There were four of them. I looked at them in the palm of my hand for a moment and then put them all, the whole dollar's worth, into my mouth at one time.

Leave to Brussels naturally entailed involved financial transactions, which helped solve the problem of the officials in charge of the disposal of used army equipment after we were discharged. A surcingle was worth fifty francs. Those straps were less than three inches wide and not very thick.

The purchasers wanted them to half-sole their shoes. A pair of army boots would bring from three to five hundred francs, depending on their age and condition. One of our boys had received a pair of hand-knitted socks for Christmas from every relative he had. They filled a sandbag. He got fifty francs a pair for them. I personally financed my Brussels leaves with socks that relatives and friends had laboured to knit, plus a big knitted muffler that was a mine of raw material. In Brussels an old lady tried to buy the gloves off my hands. They were good kid gloves, part of a Christmas parcel from someone who had heard that I was to go away for my commission in November. (The Kaiser heard that, too, and immediately abdicated.) The nice old lady offered me the equivalent of forty dollars for those gloves and was quite disappointed when I refused the offer.

One of our boys made what I have always thought was the best deal of all. He took fifty francs to the canteen where he bought cigarettes at five cents a package, the price, without excise, to servicemen. He put his two hundred packages in a sandbag and carried them to Brussels, where he sold them for twenty-five to thirty cents a package to dealers on the black market.

Going to bed in the leave centre in Brussels was quite an undertaking. The leave centre was in the old Galleries Luxembourg, a peacetime department store, which the Germans had converted into a hospital. The acres of beds left behind in floor-wide, open wards made an ideal leave centre. There was only one drawback. There were hundreds of men from scores of units, all governed by the army code that said that all army property was in the public domain and that no matter in whose possession it might be it was all legitimate loot. Add to that the fact that the men were all underfinanced for a big time on leave and were in a city that was starved for consumer goods, and you have some idea of the atmosphere of the Galleries Luxembourg.

The first thing you did when retiring was to place one leg of the cot in each boot. No doubt heavy sleepers still lost their boots but I did not see it happen. As each article of clothing was removed it was placed under the mattress. Then you could not be deprived of the government property in your possession without being disturbed. Most of us went to bed in our underwear but a few, captivated by hospital cots, stripped off completely. I have no idea of the going price of a suit of army underwear in Brussels but I know it must have been attractive to a seller, with or without livestock. I have tried to picture the scenes when the leave centre was first opened and before the protective system I have described was common practice. Imagine waking up on leave with nothing in the world except your pass and the money in your wallet. Money, of course, was not in the public domain and would probably be safe. In a crowded leave centre, however, there were no doubt some men who might not even respect a wallet. In the early days of the leave centre some innocent, no doubt, woke up naked and without either pass or money.

Food, as I have said, was controlled and I do not remember what we had to pay for a meal. If it had been exorbitant and in line with what we had to pay for uncontrolled goods I am sure that I would have remembered. In spite of controls the menus in restaurants were fascinating. My first meal in Brussels was in a large, flashy café near the Gare du Nord. The menu included chicken, goose, turkey and half a dozen kinds of meat. There was a large party of us from the battery and, just to show how tastes vary, we ordered about two-thirds of the items. My *noix de veau* was the first served and the waiter who brought it also brought my neighbour's order of turkey. We were quite surprised at how alike our plates looked. All the other plates when they arrived were exactly the same. It looked like beef and in fact tasted like it, but with a sweetish flavour. And, boy, was mine tough! We concluded that what we had was horsemeat. My only reservation is that it may have been mule. We knew, of course, that horsemeat was a common article of food on the Continent. We had seen many butcher shops with a horse's head over the door, and as we followed the retreating Germans, we had seen many dead horses by the roadside, from which large roasts had been cut before they were abandoned by their former owners. But, so far as I know, Brussels was the only place where I ever ate horse, or mule.

Only once did I wire home for money when going on leave. That was just before my first leave. When I heard what happened when the cable arrived I resolved never to cable again. For some minutes my family stood around the envelope lying on the table before anyone had the courage to open it. They did not know that what they thought was in that envelope would have come to them by telegram from Ottawa and not by cable from overseas.

My last leave was after the armistice and took me out of France for good. I had no idea of that at the time, for my pass was only for two weeks. Before that leave was over I made application to read law at the Temple under the Khaki College scheme and for the next four weeks I took daily steps to get the application approved. Every morning at nine I saw some colonel and was told to see some other colonel somewhere else the next morning at nine. Then I was free for the day, except for weekly visits to Headquarters to have my pass extended on the strength of the pending application and occasional but irregular calls at the pay office for further advances from my accumulated deferred pay. There I had an unusual, almost unprecedented reserve. When I got my third stripe and my jumping instructions after Passchendaele, I replaced a sergeant who for eighteen months had held acting rank only, without pay. My appointment was dated back to the time of his provisional stripe and my pay book was credited with eighteen months' sergeant's pay that someone else had earned and most of which I spent in London. After I had been in London nearly six weeks the battery reached England on the way home. I said, "To hell with Khaki College," and rejoined the battery. Soon I was home with the souvenir I picked up with my second-hand blankets at Witley Camp.

For that last leave I went first to Brussels and spent the night there. At six the next morning I boarded the Paris Express, which I was to leave at Lille, to take another train to Boulogne. The distance from Brussels to Lille is about eighty miles. Long stretches of the roadbed were in such bad shape that the train barely crawled. I had a battery signaller with me and when we got tired we would get out and walk beside the train. Sometimes we had to wait for it to catch up to us. There was no food on the train and there were no stops for meals. By the time we got to Lille we were very hungry.

Lille proved to be little more than a ghost town. There was no leave centre or canteen. The civilians were living on the scantiest of rations and there was not an eating place open in the whole city. We walked the snow-covered streets for an hour or more trying to find an *estaminet* which had an egg or a piece of cheese or even a slice of bread to spare for a stranger. We tried a few private houses. It was always the same story. The night of the acorn-chicory coffee was far in the past and, in all fairness, why should a civilian who probably had no more in the house than would provide breakfast share that little with a couple of well-fed soldiers who, at the worst, were only going to miss one meal? What did that matter to a person who had missed many meals and might easily miss many more?

Finally we went back to the railway station to wait for the Boulogne train. We were comforted by the fact that we would be able to eat at Boulogne and would soon be enjoying the fleshpots of London—London, where we had to produce a ration ticket to get sugar for our tea. It was midnight when we reached Boulogne. Here again there was no leave centre or canteen. We went looking for a meal. By that time everything was closed. Soon we resigned ourselves to the fact that we would have to go supperless to bed. That was unwarranted optimism; we did not even go to bed.

After banging on the doors of several *estaminets* without success we finally got one sleepy proprietor to open up for us. He had no vacant beds but he did let us sleep in his public room. That was my last night in France. We turned in supperless, not to mention lunchless and dinnerless, rolled up in our greatcoats on beer tables. I had left my kit and tin hat at the station and had nothing usual for a pillow. My pillow for my last night in France consisted of my knee-length boots, the kind that the artillery and cavalry wore in winter.